Habermas and Literary Rationality

T0383548

Routledge Studies in Contemporary Philosophy

Habermas and Literary Rationality

David L. Colclasure

Routledge
Taylor & Francis Group

NEW YORK AND LONDON

First published 2010
by Routledge
711 Third Avenue, New York, NY 10017

Simultaneously published in the UK
by Routledge
2 Park Square, Milton Park, Abingdon, Oxon OX14 4RN

Routledge is an imprint of the Taylor & Francis Group, an informa business

First issued in paperback 2013

Typeset in Sabon by Taylor & Francis Books.

Library of Congress Cataloging in Publication Data
Colclasure, David L.
  Habermas and literary rationality / by David L. Colclasure.
    p. cm. – (Routledge studies in contemporary philosophy ; 20)
  Includes bibliographical references (p.) and index.
  1. Habermas, Jürgen. 2. Literature–Philosophy. 3. Literature and society. 4. Hilbig, Wolfgang, 1941-2007. Ich. I. Title.
  B3258.H324C63 2010
  193–dc22
                           2009049989

ISBN13: 978-0-415-99471-2 (hbk)
ISBN13: 978-0-203-84954-5 (ebk)
ISBN13: 978-0-415-84810-7 (pbk)

Contents

Acknowledgements

I would like to acknowledge Beacon Press (US) and Polity Press (UK) for their permission to cite their translation of the two volumes of *Theory of Communicative Action* by Jürgen Habermas in this volume. For the purposes of this volume, I cite the Beacon Press edition with its pagination:

The Theory of Communicative Action, Volume I: Reason and the Rationalization of Society, Jürgen Habermas. Introduction and English translation Copyright © 1984 by Beacon Press. Translated by Thomas McCarthy. Originally published as *Theorie des kommunikativen Handelns: Handlungsrationalität und gesellschaftliche Rationalisierung*, Copyright © 1981 by Suhrkamp Verlag, Frankfurt. Reprinted by permission of Beacon Press, Boston.

The Theory of Communicative Action, Volume II: Lifeworld and System: A Critique of Functionalist Reason, Jürgen Habermas. Translator's preface and English translation Copyright © 1987 by Beacon Press. Translated by Thomas McCarthy. Originally published as *Theorie des kommunikativen Handelns: Zur Kritik der funktionalistischen Vernunft*, Copyright © 1981 by Suhrkamp Verlag, Frankfurt. Reprinted by permission of Beacon Press, Boston.

1 Introduction

1.1 BACKGROUND: HABERMAS ON LITERATURE AND HABERMAS ON GERMAN UNIFICATION

Taken as a whole, Jürgen Habermas's work displays a peculiar ambivalence toward literature. In his early *Structural Transformation of the Public Sphere*[1] Habermas had stressed the central historical role that the literary public sphere had played in the development of a political public sphere. There Habermas describes the development of the modern public sphere as a result of the becoming independent of capitalist economy from state authority. The beneficiaries of this development inhabited two spheres: the public and private spheres, respectively. The private sphere was centered on the institution of the bourgeois family and was secured by the economic independence of its patriarch. In the public sphere, differences in the social status of its constituent members (ideally) were irrelevant, and their inter-action consisted in the unrestricted and reasoned discussion of matters of general concern. The political aspect of the public sphere lay in the ratio-nalization of political domination by making the state accountable to (at least part of) the population. Habermas is careful to note the constitutive role that literary circles, in the form of coffeehouse literary discussions and literary journals, for instance, in the formation of the modern public sphere.

Extending Habermas's account, Peter Uwe Hohendahl argues that the eventual formation of an explicitly political public sphere relied, historically, on the "sublimated" political aspect of the earlier literary public sphere. Subject to the strictures of censorship, the interrogation of stereotypes and identities within the early literary public sphere had constituted a discreet negotiation of otherwise explicitly ideologically charged issues and cleared the way for later official institutions of public political discourse.[2] More recently, Habermas has cited and endorsed Leo Löwenthal's thesis that the institution of bourgeois literature was, by virtue of its utopic content, and from its beginning, a central mode of normative public discourse.[3] Finally, in an essay published in 1998, Habermas argues for the understanding of parti-cular Germanist conventions (*Germanistenkongresse*) as vital contributors to the political public sphere in the years before and after 1848.[4]

This positive appraisal of the societal role of literature seems to stand in contradiction, however, with the account of literature found in Habermas's theoretical work. In *TCA,* Habermas develops a theory of society in which literature, as an aesthetic practice, belongs foremost to the sphere of *expressive rationality.* Habermas considers aesthetic practice and aesthetic criticism in the modern age as concerned primarily with the genuineness of subjective self-representations. In *TCA* Habermas essentially reduces aesthetic, and hence literary, rationality to expressive rationality. This reduction is a consequence of Habermas's reduction of the claim of aesthetic *validity* to a form of the truthfulness claim. Such a line of argumentation has serious consequences for the societal role of literature, as I later demonstrate. It is surprising that Habermas gives the account of aesthetic practice and criticism in *TCA* that he does. Given his earlier emphasis of the historical role of the literary public sphere in the development of a political public sphere, why does he now restrict literary rationality to the realm of autonomous art and a concern for the truthfulness of subjective self-expression? I maintain that this restriction is an effect of oversystematization in Habermas's tripartite model of communicative action. Given the normative basis of his work taken as a whole, Habermas clearly endorses the central role of the literary public not only in the cultural but also in the political public sphere.

The inconsistency of these positions in Habermas can be particularly well illustrated, and resolved, against the background of German unification and German literature since and about unification. Although Habermas does not directly address post-unification German literature, two aspects of his publications since unification make evident the need to reconsider his account of the relation between the literary and political public spheres: (1) his exchange with and remarks on literary figures; and (2) his more recent political essays.

Habermas's dialogue with Christa Wolf, a writer from the former German Democratic Republic (GDR), is representative of the first of these aspects.[5] In their exchange of letters, Habermas disagrees with what he sees to be Wolf's dangerous drawing of continuities between the situation of intellectuals in East and West Germany as a common bias in their respective intellectual traditions. In her reply, Wolf concedes the importance of differentiating between the cultural and social conditions under which intellectuals in East and West lived. Wolf understands Habermas's critique as a useful point of departure for further discussion and is most interested in Habermas's account of his own intellectual development in West Germany. Wolf views such telling of personal stories as vital to the dialogue between East and West. In essays and interviews Habermas often refers to Christa Wolf in the context of the German–German literary controversy (the so-called *deutsch-deutscher Literaturstreit*) of 1990,[6] and in his general remarks on her status as a public intellectual it is clear that he holds the interrelation between literary and political public spheres as a considerable and productive imbrication, particularly in post-unification Germany.

Concerning the second of the aforementioned aspects, Habermas is one of many public intellectuals whose political interventions in the years following the reunification of Germany were strongly critical of the mode and tempo of the formal unification of the two German states. In numerous essays and interviews,[7] Habermas has given an account of the stark normative deficits of the political and economic fusion of the two Germanies and was early to forecast the asymmetries between East and West that would be both aggravated and produced by the hastiness of their union. In his view, German unification was an administrative act on the part of the West German federal government (*Bundesregierung*) that was carried out under the pretense of serving necessity and that grounded its legitimacy not in an informed public discussion of its conditions and consequences but rather in popular sentiments.

Beyond the clear economic disadvantages to be expected by the rash currency, political, and economic union of the two Germanies, Habermas saw the greatest deficiency of the actual mode of unification in its lack of provision for an independent political public sphere in the former GDR. Such an autonomous political public sphere would have enabled a discussion on and a determination of the political physiognomy of unified Germany on the part of all concerned:

> We would not only give up the chance to improve upon a good constitution, in its own time admittedly not legitimized by referendum, we would also pass up the historical opportunity to execute a process of a unification of the state with a clear political consciousness of the establishment of a nation of citizens.[8]

This failure is illustrated for Habermas by the quick snuffing out of forums of political public discussion represented, for instance, by the roundtable debates on the territory of the former GDR, in which East German literary figures played a constitutive role. In all of this, it is safe to say that Habermas's publications on the topic of German unification exemplify the kind of critical interventions made by a large and vocal segment of leftist-oriented public intellectuals in post-unification Germany.

What set Habermas aside from his contemporaries in the discussion of the impoverishment of the political public sphere in post-unification Germany was not merely his presence as one of the most recognized public intellectuals of his time. What ultimately distinguished him, and what simultaneously makes him interesting from a literary perspective on post-unification Germany, is the account of the role of the *literary public sphere* that can be read out of, but against the grain of, his theoretical work. Although Habermas does not give an explicit account of the literary public sphere in post-unification Germany, his theory of communicative action, when revised, provides for such an account. Moreover, a revision of the theory of communicative action to include a literary form of rationality would furnish an exceptionally convincing account of the contemporary societal role of literature in general. The particular context of post-unification Germany is useful for my argument to the extent that Habermas's essays, open letters, and interviews show a concern for the interrelation between the literary and political public spheres, a concern that necessitates a reconsideration of the underdeveloped potential of literary rationality in his theory of communicative action.

1.2   THE AIM OF A HABERMASIAN SOCIAL PHILOSOPHY OF LITERATURE

I argue that the literary public sphere, as an overlapping of the political and cultural public spheres, operates under presuppositions of a peculiar form of aesthetic rationality, namely, literary rationality. Literary rationality, I argue, provides a singular kind of impulse in the public sphere at large, an impulse which consists in the public articulation—through language—of a paradigmatic and hence shared, or shareable, *experience*. This literary form of aesthetic rationality makes complex validity claims that motivate public discussion in a way unavailable to nonliterary forms of communication. Such a conception of the literary public sphere is important in the context of post-unification German literature because it lets us give an account of precisely what is at stake in the public presentation and discussion of this particular literature. To clarify, I do not argue that the literary public in post-unification Germany was radically different from other instances of the literary public, or even historically unique in its structure; rather, I want to demonstrate that the peculiar role that the literary public can play in the public sphere at large was *particularly evident in post-unification Germany*. On the basis of a well-known post-unification novel widely hailed as an aesthetic success, I want to demonstrate the irreducibly normative content of literature on unification and its public discussion. This conclusion is not meant to refer only to the particular situation of German literature since and about unification. Rather, my ultimate aim is to provide an argument for the thesis that the peculiarity of literary rationality, and hence that of the literary public sphere, consists in the intersubjective negotiation of a complex claim of *authenticity*.

Such a social philosophy of literature can be provided for, as mentioned above, by means of a revision of Habermas's theory of communicative action. By *social philosophy of literature* I mean a description of the societal function served by the production, critique, and reception of written texts which at least implicitly lay claim to being aesthetically well-formed, which amounts, I argue, to a claim of authenticity. The specific societal function that the institutionalized practices of literature serve, is, I argue, the provision of a distinct, literary public sphere. As part of both the cultural and political public spheres, this literary public sphere plays a unique role in the articulation of matters of general concern, by virtue of its own form of rationality and its peculiar capacity to invigorate public discussion. Habermas would likely not disagree with my thesis concerning the peculiarity of literary culture. But my disagreement with Habermas concerns his account of the rationality that operates through literary language. As indicated earlier, Habermas tends to reduce literary rationality to the raising, critique, and redemption of *truthfulness* claims, which center on the transparency of subjective self-representation, i.e. genuine self-expression. I counter:

1. that aesthetic, and more specifically, literary rationality is more complex than this (more exactly, that there is no reason at all to hold the truthfulness claim as the primary kind of validity claim raised and contested through the operation of literary rationality); and
2. that literary rationality serves a function in public discussion *required* by the well-functioning public sphere.

Concerning the first sub-argument, I will demonstrate the irreducibility of the claim of aesthetic validity to any one of the three fundamental forms of validity that Habermas identifies (or even to any combination of these). This strand of my argument will take up most of the central chapter (3.1–3.2) on *TCA* and subsequent alternate accounts of aesthetic rationality.

I will then use the results of this discussion in order to demonstrate the second assertion. I take up this second sub-argument in the final section of the central chapter (3.3). At this point, I want only to roughly characterize this part of the argument, which will support the central thesis of my study. I have already mentioned that in *STPS* literature plays an important historical role in the eventual formation of the modern form of the political public sphere. Habermas does not argue there that the literary public sphere is a *conceptually necessary* component of the public sphere. Rather, his historical account illustrates the *contingent role* of literature in the development of the modern public sphere. I do not counter by arguing that the literary public sphere is in fact a conceptually necessary component of the public sphere. In fact, it is not. I do hold, however, that literature's relation to the public sphere is not merely one of historical priority. (Habermas would also not endorse such a view.) To be sure, literature has been a contingent player in the public sphere and to this extent the literary institution itself is substitutable. But the *function* that literary rationality serves (has traditionally served) in the public sphere is by no means a contingent one.

My argument will run like this: whereas literature's relation to the public sphere is not merely one of historical priority, and conversely, whereas literary culture itself is not a requirement of a well-functioning public sphere, literary culture does fill a capacity necessary to the well-functioning public sphere: the communicative use of language in an aesthetic form. This argument is weaker than it may first seem: I do not want to argue that any well-functioning public sphere must include a literary public sphere but rather that the *function* that literature serves in the public sphere is a *practically* necessary component of the well-functioning public sphere. My argument is not a preferability argument but rather an effectiveness argument. My study describes the exceptional capacity of literature to articulate *ways of considering matters of generalizable concern*. Giving such an account of the peculiarity of literary rationality is the goal that a Habermasian social philosophy of literature sets itself.

2 The Theory of Communicative Action

A Synopsis

The larger argument regarding literature's function in the public sphere outlined in the preceding, introductory chapter needs to be preceded by an account of the literary form of aesthetic rationality. Therefore I turn first to a description and evaluation of Habermas's account of aesthetic rationality. This chapter focuses on describing those aspects of Habermas's theory of communicative action relevant to any theory of aesthetic rationality, and hence to any theory of literary rationality. Although remarking in passing on contentious issues, I will reserve the elaboration of my criticism for the following chapter.

The theory of communicative action relies on a complex notion of human reason that includes several forms of rationality. The arguments presented through the exercise of these distinct forms of rationality substantiate different kinds of validity claims with different kinds of support. In contrast to theoretical or practical arguments, for instance, which establish truth or correctness claims, *aesthetic critique* establishes the appropriateness of (culturally specific) value standards: "[Aesthetic criticism] is a variation of a form of argumentation in which the adequacy of value standards, the vocabulary of our evaluative language generally, is made thematic."[1]

In aesthetic critique, according to Habermas, the kind of validity claim primarily at stake is one of the truthfulness of an (artistic) expression of experience, i.e. authenticity: "In this context reasons have the peculiar function of *bringing us to see* a work or performance in such a way that it can be perceived as an authentic expression of an exemplary experience, in general as the embodiment of a claim to authenticity."[2]

It is important to note that in Habermas's account aesthetic arguments are held to be less forceful than practical or theoretical arguments: according to Habermas, a work validated by an aesthetic argument itself becomes an argument for the acceptance of the value standards according to which the work is considered authentic.[3] Habermas thus suggests an immanent *circularity* in aesthetic argumentation. Whereas such a mode of argumentation is indeed circular, I hold that there is no reason to assume aesthetic argumentation always aims to uphold only culturally specific value standards: I will later show that the authenticity claim that Habermas himself suggests in this context has normative and descriptive aspects. Aesthetic rationality cannot be reduced, I argue, to faithful self-representation, either that of an individual (the truthfulness claim) or that of a particular culture (the authenticity claim, as Habermas understands it in the above citations).

In order to describe the system of the aforementioned types of validity claims, Habermas deploys a theory of argumentation that captures three analytical levels thereof: the levels of *process, procedure,* and *product.* On the level of process, Habermas cites the intention of argumentation to convince a *universal audience;* on the level of procedure, he cites the intention to complete a debate about hypothetical validity claims with a *rationally motivated agreement;* and on the level of product, he cites the intention to ground *with arguments* or *redeem* a validity claim.[4] Furthermore, the *kind* of validity claim primarily at stake in a proposition is detectable only given the context of that proposition's utterance. Habermas argues for three and only three universal validity claims: cognitive truth, normative rightness, and subjective truthfulness. Different forms of argumentation (theoretical, practical, and aesthetic) correspond to these different kinds of validity claims. Habermas argues that these validity claims are universal because, although recognizable only given the context of an utterance, the validity claims are not themselves constituted by the contexts.[5] Habermas hence holds that an adequate theory of argumentation must be able to describe a system of *transcendent* validity claims.

Along this line, Habermas reconstructs the raising of validity claims (at least) implicit in every speech act and describes the possible responses to this raising of validity claims. A validity claim amounts to the assertion that the validity conditions of an utterance are satisfied, i.e. *truth* for propositions, *rightness/correctness* for the description of an action or maxim of action, or *truthfulness* for an expression of subjective experience. A listener can either affirm, negate, or forbear judgment with regard to a validity claim. Habermas argues that although the *semantic* analysis of statement *forms,* which assesses (1) descriptive, (2) normative, (3) evaluative, or (4) explicative content in accordance with (1) the truth of a proposition, (2) the correctness or justifiability of a mode of action, (3) the appropriateness of certain value standards, and (4) the comprehensibility or well-formedness of symbolic representations, clarifies the validity conditions of a proposition, the formal semantic approach is—alone—insufficient for analyzing the possibility of grounding the validity of *particular* utterances.

For this, one must include the *pragmatic* component as well, Habermas argues, because what "grounding an argument" means depends on the kind of proposition in question:

> "Grounding" descriptive statements means establishing the existence of states of affairs; "grounding" normative statements, establishing the acceptability of actions or norms of action; "grounding" evaluative

statements, establishing the preferability of values; grounding expressive statements, establishing the transparency of self-presentations; and "grounding" explicative statements, establishing that symbolic expressions have been produced correctly.[6]

Important for my argument is the fact that Habermas distinguishes here between the grounding of *evaluative* utterances on the one hand and the grounding of *expressive* utterances on the other. Both of these modes of grounding are at work in aesthetic rationality, as Habermas had earlier described it, but later on in his argument, Habermas is content to subsume aesthetic rationality under mere *expressive rationality,* which consists in the raising, contestation, and redemption of truthfulness claims. This reduction leads to an inadequate account of aesthetic rationality, as I later demonstrate.

At an early stage in his argument, Habermas points out the peculiarity of truthfulness claims: "The sincerity of expressions cannot be *grounded* but only *shown;* insincerity can be *revealed* by the lack of consistency between an utterance and the past or future actions internally connected with it."[7]

This peculiarity is essential to the role that aesthetic rationality can play in Habermas's theory of communicative reason, because the truthfulness claim, for which art, for Habermas, is the paradigmatic case, *cannot be redeemed with arguments alone.* This is not the case for truth or correctness claims, which can indeed be redeemed through argumentation alone, theoretical or moral argumentation, for instance.

With particular reference to aesthetic critique, where the appropriateness of certain value standards is at stake, Habermas describes the peculiarity of aesthetic argumentation thus: "[In aesthetic argumentation] the peculiar role of arguments in this case is to open the eyes of the participants, that is, to *lead* them to an authenticating aesthetic experience."[8]

Here Habermas again seems to be suggesting that aesthetic argumentation lacks rigor, linking it to *effectiveness* and not to conviction. Furthermore, Habermas distinguishes the validity claims primarily at stake in aesthetic critique from cognitive and normative validity claims by arguing that such claims are not *universal* validity claims in a strict sense (as are, by contrast, those deployed in theoretical, practical, and explicative discourses). This is so, he argues, because aesthetic arguments presuppose a common store of values among recipients, but among only a specific group. Habermas claims here that aesthetic *critiques* are by their nature grounded by culturally specific value standards, and hence nonuniversalizable, whereas *discourses* (theoretical, practical, and explicative) are not culturally specific,[9] although he does not give an example of this kind of (aesthetic) critique. It is clear why Habermas would characterize the validity claims of aesthetic argumentation as mere critique and not as partaking in a discourse (i.e. as nonuniversalizable), if what is at stake in aesthetic arguments were in fact only culturally specific value standards. There is no reason to assume that this an adequate account of aesthetic rationality, however, as I later argue.

Habermas supplements his provisional definition of communicative rationality with a three-world conception. These "three worlds" represent three categories of knowledge, three ways of referring to the world, and are symbolically embodied in (performative) utterances: the *objective,* the *social,* and the *subjective* worlds constitute for Habermas a system of worlds that reflect the ways in which a subject can relate to "the" world through the descriptive, appellative, and expressive uses of language, respectively. Three traditional conceptions of action correspond to these three worlds: the teleological or strategic concept of action, the norm-regulated concept of action, and the dramaturgical concept of action. The *teleological* concept action turns on a decision between alternatives of action, which is determined by maxims and an interpretation of the situation, and aims at the *realization of a goal.* The teleological concept becomes a *strategic* concept of action when at least one other goal-pursuing actor is included in the success calculus (e.g., utilitarianism). The *norm-regulated* concept of action turns, in contrast, on the obedience of a *generalized norm,* the fulfillment of a legitimately expected behavior (e.g., role theory).

Most important for my argument is the concept of *dramaturgical* action, which turns on the self-representation of the subject before an audience of others. Dramaturgical action is, for Habermas, the control of public access to one's own subjectivity, and hence "[does not signify] spontaneous expressive behavior, but stylizing the expression of one's own experiences with a view to the audience."[10] Habermas wants to separate his own conception of communicative action from all three of these fundamental concepts of action (when these operate in isolation) by focusing on (1) the *undertaking of an interpersonal relationship* through communicative interaction and (2) the *coordination of plans of actions* through the (3) *shared interpretation of a situation.*[11] Habermas's communicative concept of action turns on an intersubjective interpretation and the possibility of a consensus regarding the definition of situations and contexts of action.[12]

Habermas has added the element of language to his provisional definition of communicative action but qualifies this addition so as to not include strategic action: each of the three basic models of action named here can be conceived in a one-sided manner, to the extent that language can be considered a means to attaining an end external it. The one-sided conception of language in dramaturgical action consists in the reduction of language to its rhetorical capacity at the expense of its descriptive and normative content. By contrast, the communicative model of action incorporates all three of the aforementioned models of action into a framework in which the strategic aspect is subsidiary to the communicative orientation of a use of language: "Only the communicative model of action presupposes language as a medium of uncurtailed communication whereby speakers and hearers, out of the context of their preinterpreted lifeworld, refer simultaneously to things in the objective, social, and subjective worlds in order to negotiate common definitions of the situation."[13]

As one would expect, given his supplementation of formal semantic analysis of statement forms with the pragmatic aspect of particular utterances, Habermas chooses not the sentence but rather the *speech act* that can be answered by at least one interaction partner with "yes" or "no" as the unit for analysis of communicative action. This he does in order to clarify the conditions of the communicative *coordination of action,* which co-constitutes the concept of communicative action. That is to say, communicative action signifies a class of interactions which are coordinated by speech acts but which are not reducible to the latter.[14] By selecting the speech act as his analytical unit, Habermas is able to productively describe paradigmatic, everyday uses of language, but this selection cannot describe nonstandard uses of language, in particular the literary use thereof. I later address how one can nonetheless extend Habermas's account of communicative action to include at least one use of language, the literary, that cannot adequately be described in terms of speech acts.

For empirical support to his theory of the distinct nature of the three types of validity claims, Habermas relies on Max Weber's theory of modernization as a process of rationalization and differentiation of autonomous spheres of rationality. Cultural rationalization in the Western world consists for Weber in the becoming independent of three spheres of validity: those of science and technology, law and morality, and art and expressive self-representation, respectively. Cultural rationalization in the broader sense consists in each of these spheres of validity beginning to follow an independent logic, on Weber's account.[15] Cultural rationalization in the narrower sense consists in the augmentation of a certain value *within* each of the respective spheres of validity.

Within the aesthetic sphere, the value augmented is *novelty* in modes of self-expression: "With regard finally to value enhancement in the aesthetic domain, the idea of progress fades into that of renewal and rediscovery, an innovative revivification of authentic experiences."[16]

Yet the cultivation of novelty does not consist merely in the developing of new techniques. It consists rather in the development of a more radical mode of self-representation, one increasingly independent from concerns for theoretical or objective truth on the one hand and moral rightness on the other hand. The point of view from which rationalization of the aesthetic sphere is possible is, Habermas argues, that of "those abstract ideas that are decisive for the inner logics of value spheres as such: [...] beauty, authenticity, sincerity in the expressive sphere of value."[17] Although Habermas here mentions beauty and authenticity as validity claims separate from truthfulness, he carries out his subsequent argument concerning aesthetic rationality as if it could be mapped entirely onto expressive rationality and the truthfulness claim with which the latter operates.

It is the rationalization of world-views in modern Western society that led to the formal conceptions of an objective, a social, and a subjective world and to the corresponding fundamental attitudes toward a cognitive and morally *objectified* outer world on the one hand and a *subjectified* inner world on the other hand, Habermas argues with Weber. Out of the combination of (1) the *objectifying* attitude and the *norm-conform* (or norm-critical) attitude toward the organization of society, and the *expressive* attitude toward the subjectivity of "inner nature"; and (2) the three formal world concepts, Habermas posits nine fundamental, formal-pragmatic, actor-world relations.[18] I cannot address all of these here. But those most important for my argument are those combinations of formal concepts of the world with the expressive attitude:

1. the expressive attitude toward the *objective world* consists in *an aesthetic relation to one's nonobjectified environment;*
2. the expressive attitude toward the *social world* consists in *self-representation;*
3. the expressive attitude toward the *subjective world* consists in a *sensual-spontaneous relation toward oneself.*[19]

These can be explained, Habermas argues, through:

1. artworks, style phenomena, and theories in which a morphological view of nature reigns;
2. social actions of the dramaturgical type;
3. affective utterances, libidinous stirrings, creative accomplishments, etc.

The expressive attitude toward both inner and outer nature constitutes "a complex of aesthetic-practical rationality, within which the production of knowledge can take the form of authentic interpretations of needs, interpretations that have to be renewed in each historically changed set of circumstances."[20] Aesthetic rationality is limited, for Habermas, to the expressive attitude toward the *subjective* world, which he cashes out in historical forms of *erotic practice* (by which he apparently means all the varied forms of self-oriented engagement with one's desires and perceived needs), and to the expressive attitude to the *objective* world, which he cashes out in the form of *artistic practice.*

But it is not merely the case that art and erotic practice have historically embodied aesthetic rationality, but rather that they are, for Habermas, instances of *the only structurally rationalizable, expressive, formal-pragmatic actor-world relations.*[21] He eliminates the expressive attitude toward the social world as a rationalizable formal-pragmatic relation, by arguing that such relations are parasitic on innovations from other (presumably theoretical and practical) value spheres. Whether or not his argument is a good one, Habermas's suggestion is clear: aesthetic artifacts and aesthetic criticism, as manifestations of expressive rationality, display no unique significance for the social world.

Indeed, Habermas indicates explicitly what he sees as the minimal social relevance of aesthetic rationality historically:

> *Aesthetic-practical rationality* is institutionalized in the artistic enterprise. Of course, autonomous art has just as little structure-forming effect on society as a whole as do the shifting, unstable countercultures that form around this subsystem. On the other hand, the extraordinary values of this sphere for the focus for a hedonistic life-style directed toward innerworldly salvation, the life-style of the "sensualist" who is acting against the "pressure of the theoretical and practical" rationality of the ordinary "specialist," who is established in science, the economy, and the state.[22]

The problem with Habermas's account here is that he limits his description of aesthetic rationality to those (avant-garde) art movements and theories of art that aim at the cultivation of a realm of aesthetic validity independent of theoretical and practical rationality. Limiting aesthetic rationality to expressive rationality in this way fails to account for the complex workings of aesthetic practice and criticism that, consciously or not, avails itself of validity claims other than that of subjective truthfulness, as I later argue. A conception of the authenticity claim that is more complex than a subjective truthfulness claim will show that Habermas's presumption of the minimal social relevance of aesthetic rationality is false, a refutation to which I will later return.

A further aspect important to an understanding of the role of aesthetic rationality in his theory of communicative action is Habermas's appropriation of analytical theories of meaning. Habermas's employs Karl Bühler's semiotic model of the use of the linguistic *signifier* (by a *sender,* in order to communicate about objects and states of affairs, to a *receiver*) and the three functions of the use of linguistic signifiers that Bühler describes: "the cognitive function of representing a state of affairs, the expressive function of making known the experiences of the speaker, and the appellative function of directing requests to addressees."[23]

Habermas is not content to settle for just any one of the three most important, traditional analytical theories of meaning (Peirce's *reference semantics,* Carnap's *logical syntax,* and Frege's, the early Wittgenstein's, and Davidson's *truth semantics*). On the basis of the later Wittgenstein's, Austin's, and Searle's development of the *use theory of meaning* and the *theory of speech acts,* Habermas wants to account for the pragmatic aspects of language use. Habermas intends to generalize Bühler's theory to include validity conditions not only on the semantic level of propositions, but also on the pragmatic level of utterances.

Habermas wants to extend the analytic theories of meaning (which focus on truth conditions) by including in his theory of communication the systematic grounding of the appellative, expressive, and the poetic functions of language:

> The theory of meaning can attain the level of integration of the communication theory that Bühler advanced in a programmatic way only if it is able to provide a systematic grounding for the appellative and expressive functions of language (and perhaps also for the "poetic" function related to the linguistic means themselves as this was developed by Jakobson), in the same way the truth-conditional semantics has done for the representational function.[24]

This mention of the "poetic function" of language does not receive any further treatment in *TCA*, but Habermas does return to it in a later article, which I will address later.[25] Here again it is curious that Habermas distinguishes between expressive and poetic uses of language—indicating a more or less independent logic of literary rationality—only to subsequently lump them together under the umbrella concept of expressive rationality.

Furthermore, central to Habermas's delimitation of communicative action is the strict separation between the success-oriented and the communication-oriented use of language, which corresponds to a strict separation of perlocutionary effects from illocutions, and hence a strict exclusion of perlocutionary effects from the class of communicative actions. Habermas makes the strong claim that success-orientation and communication-orientation are not merely two analytical aspects of any given speech act but rather that they can be distinguished under appropriate circumstances on the basis of the intuitive knowledge of the speakers.[26] Habermas goes on to argue that the communication-oriented use of language is the *original mode* of language use. Habermas will ultimately support this claim by using Austin's distinction between illocutionary and perlocutionary speech acts. Austin had distinguished between (1) locutionary, (2) illocutionary, and (3) perlocutionary speech acts, which correspond, respectively, to (1) saying something; (2) acting, by saying something; and (3) bringing about an effect, through acting, by saying something.[27]

Habermas dedicates a considerable amount of argumentation to establishing the distinction between perlocutionary and illocutionary speech acts. Whereas an illocution is clear from the constitutive meaning of what is said itself, the perlocution is only understandable on the basis of the speaker's *intention*. And, at best, the speaker's intention can be taken from the context of the utterance. In an illocution *the conditions for success* of the speech act are deducible from the speech act itself; those of a perlocution extend beyond the speech act. An illocution is successful when the listener accepts an *assertion as true,* or when the listener accepts an *appeal as correct.* In the second case, acceptance grounds *obligations of action* on the listener's part, and *expectations of action* on the speaker's part.

The perlocutionary speech act is, for Habermas, one in which an illocutionary speech act is connected (by the speaker) with a purpose (a teleological action).[28] Habermas also accepts a further criterion from Strawson, in order to underscore the distinction between perlocutionary effects and pure illocutions: *perlocutionary goals cannot be revealed*, if one wants to succeed; *illocutionary goals are only achieved if one pronounces them*, i.e. makes them explicit. Habermas hence defines perlocutionary speech acts as those speech acts which use an illocution in order to achieve an effect not determinable on the basis of the illocution alone, while not revealing the intended goal of the speech act (I later discuss Habermas's subsequent revision of this definition).

Finally, Habermas substantiates his argument that the communicative use of language is the original mode of language use with the following argument:

> If the hearer failed to understand what the speaker was saying, a strategically acting speaker would not be able to bring the hearer, by means of communicative acts, to behave in the desired way. To this extent, what we initially designated as "the use of language with an orientation to consequences" is not an original use of language.[29]

Perlocutionary effects, and hence perlocutionary uses of illocutions are thus strictly excluded from the class of communicative actions: "What we mean by reaching understanding has to be clarified *solely* in connection with illocutionary acts."[30] This is a further restriction on the definition of communicative action: that all participants pursue their illocutionary goals *without reserve*: "I have called the type of interaction in which *all* participants harmonize their individual plans of action with one another and thus pursue their illocutionary aims *without reservation* 'communicative action'."[31] Those interactions in which at least one of the participants pursues the realization of perlocutionary effects is considered by Habermas to be "linguistically mediated strategic action."[32] I will later challenge Habermas's distinction between illocutions and perlocutionary effects, not by arguing that these are always concomitant but rather by arguing that the distinction itself neglects another class of "effects" of speech acts: those effects which are neither specified in a particular illocution, nor are merely the effect of a strategic deployment of illocutions. Such a reclassification is necessary, I show, in order to account for certain "effects" of the literary use of language by means of which the literary public sphere extends into the political public sphere.

The limitation of communicative action to the binding effect of illocutions is significant to Habermas's theory of communicative action because it determines the *relation between meaning and validity of speech acts*. When a listener accepts the validity claim of a speech act with a "yes," he/she grounds a communicative exchange that refers on the one hand to the *content of the utterance* and on the other hand to *speech-immanent guarantees* and *obligations concerning the consequences of that interaction.*[33] Habermas distinguishes three levels of reaction of the listener's side:

1. He/she understands the expression.
2. He/she takes a position on it (yes/no), i.e. accepts it or not.
3. He/she directs his/her action according to it (i.e. according to conventionally established obligations of action).

The communicative act is precisely the (successful) connection of these three levels of response: "The *pragmatic* level of agreement that is effective for coordination [2] connects the *semantic* level of understanding meaning [1] with the *empirical* level of developing further—in a manner dependent on the context—the accord relevant to the sequel of interaction [3]."[34]

Habermas delineates two ways of making this connection effective. He argues that one understands a speech act when one knows the conditions of acceptability of its illocutionary success. These conditions must be *intersubjectively recognized*, and, if so, ground obligations concerning the consequences of the communicative interaction. The first way of making this connection effective, in the case of a regulative use of language, for instance, is with an imperative. An imperative is backed up by a claim to power over the listener. Or, a command can be backed up normatively, by a validity claim, which is not the expression of a contingent will, as is a claim to power over the listener. Only the second case is one of *rational motivation* of the listener to accept a speech act:

> We are now in a position to say that a speaker can *rationally motivate* to accept his speech act offer because—on the basis of an internal connection between validity, validity claim, and redemption of a validity claim—he can assume the *warranty* [*Gewähr*] for providing, if necessary, convincing reasons that would stand up to a hearer's criticism of the validity claim. Thus a speaker owes the binding (or bonding: *bindende*) force of his illocutionary act not to the validity of what is said but to the *coordinating effect of the warranty* that he offers: namely to redeem, if necessary, the validity claim raised by his speech act.[35]

Rational motivation of another takes the place of empirical sanctioning when the illocutionary role of the speech act expresses not a claim to power, but rather a validity claim. To show that a given practice is an ultimately rationally grounded practice, one must be able to describe the contestable validity claims raised in it. To show that a given practice is a form of communicative *action*, one must be able to describe the way that the raising of such contestable validity claims has an action-coordinating effect. In this context, my argument will aim at describing the (peculiar) validity claim in the literary institution and showing that the validity claims at work in the literary institution have an action-coordinating effect.

Habermas argues that the coordination of action on the basis of validity claims is not only part of regulative speech acts but also of expressive and constative speech acts:

> Thus a hearer understands [an] avowal [of loathing] if he knows (a) the conditions under which a person under which a person could experience loathing for *p,* and (b) the conditions under which *S* says what he means and thereby accepts responsibility for the consistency of his further behavior with this confession.[36]

Yet there exists an important asymmetry between expressive speech acts and regulative speech acts. Understanding an expressive speech act does not include recognizing any (strong) obligations of action but rather only recognizing the conditions under which a statement may be regarded as truthful. Obligation of action result from expressive speech acts only to the extent that the speaker *specifies that with which his behavior may not con-tradict:* "That a speaker means what he says can be made credible only in the consistency of what he does and not through providing grounds."[37] Indeed, Habermas makes the strong argument that *only* truthfulness claims have *immediate* relevance for the continuation of the communicative inter-action at hand: "[t]hey contain an offer of the hearer to check against the consistency of the speakers past or future sequence of actions whether he means what he says."[38] Because Habermas subsumes aesthetic rationality under expressive rationality, he thus implies that the aesthetic critique con-sists in some form in a test of the correspondence of an aesthetic artifact with its creator's pattern of actions. But this hardly promises a satisfactory account of the evaluative criteria at work in aesthetic critique, as I later elaborate.

The second volume of *TCA* contains some important references to the literary sphere and the aesthetic sphere in general that should be mentioned here. Habermas's appropriation of Weber's theory of modernization as rationalization had made clear that the rationalization of the lifeworld had simultaneously (1) set off the differentiation of independent cultural subsystems (science/technology, art/aesthetic practice, and law/morality) *and* (2) opened up a division between public and private spheres, in which a utopian, socially critical potential could be cultivated. Habermas notes that in the self-understanding of eighteenth-century bourgeois society, art and literature were central vehicles for the critical potential of communication-oriented action.[39] The *"appearance of posttraditional everyday communication"*[40] which, among other cultural institutions, literature exhibited, promised a utopian potential that remained unrealized. Habermas does not agree that either rationalization itself or the becoming independent of cultural subsystems was the cause of this failure. Responsible for this failure is rather "an elitist splitting-off of expert cultures from contexts of communicative action in daily life,"[41] i.e. the penetration of the media of money and administrative power into systems of action that must nonetheless specialize in cultural tradition, social integration and education, and which rely on communication as the mechanism of the coordination of action (of which literature is a clear example).[42]

In his account of the goals of any critical theory of society (of which *TCA* is an attempt), Habermas indicates the latter's perspective on the phenomena of mass media and mass culture. A critical theory of society "makes us skeptical of the thesis that the essence of the public sphere has been liquidated in postliberal societies."[43] Mass media are not, on Habermas's account, merely steered by the media of money and administrative power but rather represent "generalized forms of communication,"[44] and, as such, do not *replace* communication, but rather *condense* and hence *remain reliant on* lifeworld contexts. Mass media—and although literature is distinct here, it nonetheless remains to some extent a mass-media phenomenon for Habermas—hence enable the formation of new forms (and forums) of publicity, i.e. of communicative rationality.

Finally, Habermas prescribes that a critical theory of society address the questions of whether the different rationalities can maintain some form of unity, and whether expert cultures can be brought back into exchange with everyday communicative practice.[45] Habermas presumes an ultimate commonality between the separate spheres of rationality: "The only protection against an empiricist abridgement of the rationality problematic is a steadfast pursuit of the tortuous routes along which science, morality and art communicate with one another."[46] Habermas entrusts post-avant-garde forms of (simultaneously realistic and politically engaged) art with the ability to mediate aspects of the cognitive and moral-practical spheres of knowledge.[47] The critical potential of such aesthetic practice lies for Habermas in its ability to cultivate a nonobjectified communicative practice: "It seems as if the radically differentiated moments of reason want in such countermovements to point toward a unity—not a unity that could be had at the level of worldviews, but one that might be established *this side* of expert cultures, in a nonreified communicative everyday practice."[48]

Clearly, the second volume of *TCA* stands in strange contrast to the first volume, to the extent that the positive appraisal of the socially critical potential of post-avant-garde art forms receives no theoretical treatment comparable to the one that the avant-garde forms of art and theories of art had in the first volume. The account of aesthetic rationality given in the first volume sees aesthetic rationality as a subsidiary form of expressive rationality, paradigmatic for which is the dramaturgical model of action, which in turn centers on a stylized self-representation that objectifies an audience, and hence cannot constitute a legitimate model of action in communicative reason. Although presented before a public, aesthetic, and hence literary practice seems to be unable to take up a significant and legitimate role in society, in Habermas's theoretical account. His account of aesthetic rationality is inadequate to the extent that it deals only with those historical manifestations of aesthetic practice, criticism, and theory that focus on expressivity. This prejudices his own account of aesthetic rationality as belonging fundamentally to expressive rationality. A consideration of other manifestations of aesthetic rationality would make it possible to consider the latter a form of communicative action. I will go about this demonstration in two steps: by (1) giving a more extensive account of aesthetic, and in particular literary, rationality than Habermas does (Chapter 3); and by (2) illustrating my description of literary rationality and substantiating the claim that it is a peculiar form of communicative action on the basis of an actual literary text and actual literary criticism (Chapter 4).

3   Literary Rationality and Communicative Reason

The foregoing chapter has prepared the following, evaluative discussion of various accounts of the relation between aesthetic rationality and communicative reason. This chapter will elaborate and support my critique of Habermas's theory of communicative action, not in order to depreciate its value as a theory of society but to challenge its account of the societal role of literature and to present an account of the latter that appreciates the communicative and action-coordinating capacity of literature and indeed the necessity of the function that literary rationality serves in the reasoning practice of the public sphere at large. This critique of Habermas will take place in three stages, each of which makes up a section in this chapter.

In the first section (3.1) I will discuss methodological and theoretical problems in revising *TCA* (and Habermas's own subsequent revisions of it) to include aesthetic rationality. The *methodological* problem (3.1.1) concerns the unit of analysis: Habermas selects the individual, "standard form" of the speech act as the basis for his analysis of communicative reason, which will clearly not work in a straightforward manner in the case of literature. The answer to this methodological problem, which consists in the *consideration of context* (in various senses of the latter term), is actually already present in Habermas in an underdeveloped form. The *theoretical* problems in *TCA* and subsequent revisions of it that are relevant to my discussion are numerous (3.1.2) and will be dealt with under three headings:

1. Habermas's *reduction of aesthetic rationality to expressive rationality,* which is demonstrable in part on the basis of his assertion of the predominance of the truthfulness claim in aesthetic practice;
2. Habermas's *correlation of truthfulness claims to the predominance of a concern for perlocutionary effects,* which is demonstrable on the basis of his discussion of certain example forms of speech acts; and
3. Habermas's definition of the peculiarity of literary language as the predominance of the "poetic function" and the concomitant *suspension of illocutionary force inherent in literary uses of language.*

I argue that Habermas's treatment of the literary use of language in particular, and aesthetic rationality in general, neglects and falsely characterizes a peculiar communicative potential that, according to the normative basis of his own theory of the public sphere, can, does, and *ought to* coordinate action outside of its immediate environment (the literary public sphere).

The second section (3.2) mobilizes alternative accounts of aesthetic validity and aesthetic rationality (Franz Koppe, Albrecht Wellmer, and Martin Seel) in order to develop a new account of the interrelation of aesthetic validity with other forms of validity and that of aesthetic rationality with other forms of rationality. My account is new because it critically assesses certain aspects of those theories of aesthetic rationality and demonstrates how Habermas's theory can be extended to include them. In particular, I agree with Koppe's understanding the articulation of subjective needs through aesthetic artifacts as inherently intersubjective but reject his ultimate adherence to Habermas's reduction of aesthetic rationality to expressive rationality: I argue that the peculiarity of aesthetic rationality lies not in a purportedly superior articulation of subjective needs (as compared to propositional or normative uses of language), as Koppe argues, but rather in its capacity to articulate *ways of looking at* the objective, social, and subjective worlds *in light of* shareable subjective experiences. I agree with Wellmer's argument for "truth" in art as a phenomenon of interference between the different dimensions of validity but reject his tendency toward an idealistic aesthetics in his account of aesthetic practice as a utopic regulative that overcomes speechlessness. With Seel, I argue for the understanding of aesthetic validity as (in part) the validity of innovative articulation of ways-the-world-is (*Weltweisenartikulation*), but against Seel I argue that the notion of aesthetic validity is not fully captured by the reorienting or capacity of art to articulate the ways-the-world-is.

I do *not* argue that the claim of aesthetic validity is redeemed in full only when its potential truth-effects are realized but rather that the claim of aesthetic validity contains irreducibly normative and assertory elements. The articulation of ways-that-the-world-is that Seel accurately describes as the peculiar contribution of aesthetic practice necessarily avails itself of claims along all three dimensions of validity: "*I* hold that this is *the right way* to look at this *situation* (i.e. these particular states of affairs that are, *objectively*, in force)." Seel wants to demonstrate how aesthetic validity also exists outside of any explicit validity claims, to the extent that aesthetic practice can result in the actual reorientation in the recipient without a thematization of the artwork's aesthetic validity claims. Against this view, I want to show aesthetic validity is not adequately described as the actuality of reorientation in the recipient. The aesthetic validity of literary artworks, I argue, lies neither in their capacity of "world-disclosure" (Wellmer) nor in their capacity of the "disclosure of world-disclosure" (Seel) alone. Rather, the claim of aesthetic validity in literature refers also to its peculiar ability to induce public discussion of issues of generalizable concern (in which truth, rightness, or truthfulness claims all play constitutive roles).

The *redemption* of the aesthetic validity claim of a piece of literature depends not on the coordination of particular actions specifiable on the basis of a particular text but rather on the consequences for subsequent actions that the *reorientation* of a recipient of a piece of literature has or could have. "Has or could have": this distinction is necessary in order to distinguish social currency (*Geltung*) from (aesthetic) validity (*Gültigkeit*)—that is, a piece of literature can be aesthetically valid even if it does not actually occasion the kind of discussion described above, a point with which Seel agrees. But the aesthetic validity, social or otherwise, of an aesthetic artifact presupposes an at-least-implicit *claim* of validity. I will argue that this claim of aesthetic validity is a claim of authenticity that contains subsidiary claims of objective, normative, and subjective validity. Whereas the claim of aesthetic validity may not be explicit in the piece of literature in question, the fact of its public appearance and its public discussion imply that it is treated as raising a validity claim, one that is substantiated (or not), on the basis of the text and the complex of views on the objective, social, and (respective) subjective worlds that it articulates. The raising and contestation of this claim of authenticity, and its endorsement or rejection, by means of arguments, is the singular but not exclusive function of aesthetic rationality.

Finally, the third section (3.3) delineates the peculiarity of literary rationality as a form of aesthetic rationality and the contribution of literary rationality to the public sphere at large. In the first subsection (3.3.1), I explain that what distinguishes the literary variety of aesthetic rationality is, trivially, its (communicative) use of language, as compared to non-linguistic systems of signification. I go on to distinguish the claim of *literary* authenticity from the criteria of (1) well-formedness and (2) the preferability of particular cultural value standards that Habermas includes in his general description of aesthetic validity. I argue that these (well-formedness and preferability of cultural value standards) have, in the case of the literary use of language, a different status than in nonliterary aesthetic critique, precisely because of the peculiar kind of language use in question. Linguistic well-formedness, for instance, which is a necessary requirement for the comprehension of a standard speech act, is neither a necessary nor a sufficient condition for qualifying as literarily well-formed (often enough the literarily well-formed is, according to traditional norms, linguistically ill-formed). What distinguishes literary from nonliterary uses of language, and hence literary from mere linguistic well-formedness, and what also renders literary rationality a form of aesthetic rationality, is the justificatory priority of the authenticity claim. And what makes literary rationality distinct from nonliterary forms of aesthetic rationality, is not just its medium (language) but what it conveys about its medium: the communicative use of language in an aesthetic form (i.e. with an authenticity claim attached to it) is a peculiar use of language because it does not just disclose issues of generalizable concern (shareable experiences), and not just because it discloses ways of looking at issues of generalizable concern, but because it discloses *ways of articulating, through language use,* issues of generalizable concern.

In the last section (3.3.2), I argue that, by means of its own form of rationality, literature and literary discourse uniquely invigorates public discussion. Literature, in particular, can do this by producing a rationally grounded *resonance* in a reading/listening public, which can result, on the basis of the complex claim of authenticity internal to the literary institution, in the *reorientation* in the recipients' view of the world. Herein lies the *practical* necessity of the literary public sphere's function in the public sphere at large: this is the larger argument that I will be building up throughout this volume. This formulation of it is neither an argument for a strong, conceptual necessity, nor a merely prescriptive, preferability argument with regard to literature's role in the public sphere. Rather, it is an effectiveness argument: the public sphere in which, on the basis of shareable, i.e. intersubjectively authentic experiences, not just issues of generalizable concern, but the validity of ways of looking at and articulating such issues is contested and negotiated, is a more *effective*, i.e. better functioning, public sphere than one in which such experiences are not reflexively experienced and publicly articulated. This is the unique contribution of the literary public sphere to the public sphere at large. I argue with Habermas that the peculiarity of the literary use of language consists in a certain kind of reflexivity, but against him that this reflexivity implies that the illocutionary force of the literary use of language is suspended. Habermas's argument that the illocutionary force of speech acts *within* literary texts indeed carries over into argument that the illocutionary force of literary texts themselves is in some significant sense suspended. This would disqualify it as a potential form of communicative action, and it is this disqualification that I intend to refute.

3.1 THE THEORY OF COMMUNICATIVE ACTION AND AESTHETIC RATIONALITY

3.1.1 The Methodological Problem: The Speech Act as Unit of Analysis

The methodological question of what unit of analysis is to be used in a consideration of the literary use of language as a form of communicative action is not so much a problem with Habermas's theory but rather a problem of applying Habermas's approach to literature. This is so because Habermas is not concerned with literature but rather with a demonstration of the communicative practice of raising and redeeming validity claims on the basis of *standard forms of everyday language,* an intention served perfectly well by a consideration of paradigmatic speech acts. Although neither literary texts nor a program for their analysis in terms of communicative action falls under the declared horizon of Habermas's theory, clues as to how the theory of communicative action might include an account of *nonstandard forms of communication-oriented speech* can be found in Habermas's approach.

As indicated in the previous chapter, for Habermas, only those speech acts that raise contestable validity claims are constitutive of communicative action: "Not all illocutionary acts are constitutive for communicative action, but only those with which speakers connect criticizable validity claims."[1] Aside from the question of the nature of criticizable validity claims raised through the literary use of language, which is a problem in its own right, it is clear that the definition of communicative action in terms of speech acts complicates an inclusion of literature in communicative action. It is evident that a text, literary or otherwise, is not a speech act as Habermas uses the term. The speech act is traditionally distinguished from the sentence by its pragmatic aspect: an adequate description of a speech act includes not only the latter's *propositional content,* but also the specific context of its *use.* According to this definition, the problem with using the term *speech act* to refer to a literary text is not so much the availability of the context of its use—this is at hand in literary histories and institutional analyses, for instance. The problem here is rather, at least on first glance, the *size* of the particular use of language involved: the literary text is clearly much larger and complex than a single sentence or utterance.

There would nonetheless be two basic, combinable strategies for analyzing a literary text in terms of speech acts, if one attempts to work with Habermas on the terms of his own, explicit definition of communicative action. I hold that neither of these strategies nor their combination is necessary, but will indicate them in order to show why my approach is the most plausible. First, one could consider a literary text to be a series of speech acts which are linked in some fashion or another and which could be analyzed individually. Second, such a text could be taken to represent a "speech act" of a different order when taken as a whole: the whole of the "work" as a nonpropositional *expression* of authorial subjectivity. A literary text could also be analyzed from both of these perspectives simultaneously: this consideration of *both the propositional and expressive content* of a literary work would match traditional attempts to (1) glean authorial "intention" (and realization or failure of that intention, i.e. the consistency or inconsistency of the propositional and expressive content); or at least to (2) represent the literary "whole which is greater than the sum of its parts." Or, alternately, it may turn out that a literary text constitutes a use of language the meaning of which is not fully captured by the term *speech act,* or even that the literary text cannot be described in terms of speech acts at all.

I hold that *whatever* the plausibility of employing the speech act as an analytical category in the case of literary texts, Habermas's theory of communicative action can still be applied to literature. That is, it is not necessary to determine either whether or how the *literary text* can be cashed out in terms of speech acts in order to describe the character of *literature* as a form of communicative action. This last claim is *prima facie* inconsistent with Habermas's definition of communicative action as including only (1) those speech acts connected, by the speaker, with (2) at least implicit, contestable validity-claims. But, of these two, the second aspect is the only strictly necessary condition of constituting communicative action. This claim will necessitate a description of the nature of the (implicit) validity claims raised through the literary use of language, which I later return to.

First, however, I want to show why the speech act *need not be* the only unit of analysis in a description of communicative action. Even on Habermas's own account, there are at least three, analytically separable, reasons that would make this claim a plausible one: (a) it may be necessary to consider larger units of discourse in order to determine whether any given individual speech act is communicative; (b) as long as all discourse participants operate under presuppositions of a communication-oriented use of language, otherwise strategic uses of language belong to communicative action; and (c) communicative action encompasses not merely speech acts themselves, but also the *context of interaction* that is created by such speech acts, and in which further action is *coordinated*. Whereas (a) specifically concerns the size of the analytical sample; (b) concerns the institutional background of the use of language in question (or *at least* the presuppositions under which the discourse participants in a particular exchange are operating); and (c) concerns the potential extra-institutional consequences of institution-internal uses of language.

3.1.1.1 Indirect Communication through Perlocutionary Effects

When discussing *strategic* uses of language, Habermas himself suggests that larger units of discourse (than individual speech acts) may have to be considered in order to sufficiently determine the status of individual elements, i.e. whether they are, in the end, communicative or merely strategic. He notes that a consideration of an "entire sequence of speech" may be necessary in order to determine the communicative potential of any individual, seemingly merely strategic elements.[2] Habermas' reason for conditionally accepting strategic elements as belonging to communicative action is the occasional necessity of "indirect communication," with which he seems to equate the strategic use of the perlocutionary effects of speech acts: "Through perlocutionary effects, the speaker gives the hearer something to understand which he cannot (yet) directly communicate."[3] Although Habermas gives no example here, he apparently means the use of a rhetorical strategy, e.g., the use of overstatement or an ironic remark, in order to introduce a topic or illustrate a problem to be discussed. Habermas conditionally accepts the strategic use of perlocutionary effects: only if what is indirectly communicated also facilitates direct communication in the larger context, does it count as belonging to communicative action. And in order to establish that the facilitation of communication is actually the more important operation of indirect uses of language, one must occasionally take into account a larger sample of the use of language in question. In the case of literature, this point is relevant to the extent that textual interpretation, as *textual* interpretation, *must* rely on meanings gleaned from a macro-perspective, and *not only* on meanings derived from individual statements.

Habermas otherwise *generally* excludes perlocutionary effects from communicative action. I will later argue that this inconsistency is in Habermas because of his distinction between illocutionary and perlocutionary effects of language use, a distinction which I intend to show to be inadequate (see 3.1.2.2). Already Habermas's concession that communicative action may, under the right circumstances, avail itself of perlocutionary effects, indicates the problematic nature of a strict, two-class division in this regard. Furthermore, the exclusion of perlocutionary effects from communicative action presupposes (1) that indirect communication and the strategic use of language are coextensive, and (2) that the actualization of perlocutionary effects (understood broadly, i.e. as Habermas does, as the effects produced by an illocutionary speech act which cannot be determined solely on the basis of the illocutionary content of a use of language) always allow one to presume a strategic use of language. I counter that there are in fact indirect uses of language that aim at what Habermas broadly defines as perlocutionary effects and that are nonetheless communicative (i.e. nonstrategic). I later argue that Habermas's subsequent (post-*TCA*) differentiation of communicative and noncommunicative classes of perlocutionary effects still does not give an adequate definition of what can count as a communicative use of language.

3.1.1.2 *Presuppositions of the Literary Institution*

The *acceptability,* for Habermas, of strategic elements in what is, overall, a communication-oriented use of language further indicates that *general institutional presuppositions* (or at least presuppositions manifest in a particular exchange) concerning form and technique must be considered when evaluating the character of a use of language as communicative or noncommunicative. As long as all participants are working under presuppositions of the communicative use of language, Habermas must be willing to accept even such institutionally specific uses of language which are partly, and even *predominantly* indirect, i.e. not analyzable into discrete speech-acts, as belonging to communicative action.[4] It seems intuitively correct to identify literature as just one such institutionally-specific and *at least partly indirect* use of language. Following this line of argument, it would be valid on Habermas's own terms to apply the theory of communicative action to the literary sphere, as long one can demonstrate that the indirect uses of language in literature can occur under presuppositions of the communicative use of language, and because what is communicated indirectly *could not be said* directly. This is a way of fitting literature into Habermas's theory that I do not take. It may well be true that what is singularly communicated by literature could not be said directly, but showing this is not necessary in order to show that institutional presuppositions render literature and literary discourse a forum for communicative action. In other words, *implicit presuppositions* are not the same as *indirect uses of language*. To show that literature and literary discourse qualify as a forum for communicative action requires only a demonstration that the former (implicit presuppositions) are communication-oriented.

3.1.1.3   *Context of Interaction of Literary Speech Acts*

Habermas stresses the "difference between a speech act and the context of interaction that it constitutes through achieving a coordination of the plans of different actors."[5] This difference lies in the fact that a speech act need not exhaust itself in its utterance, but may also serve as a *coordinating mechanism for further actions*. To the extent that one can demonstrate that the literary use of language creates a context of interaction through which extra-institutional action may be coordinated (political activism, as a more manifest example, but also a "mere" change in *attitude* of the recipient that has or could have substantial consequences); and as long as the interactional relation created among participants is based on contestable validity claims, the question whether literature is reducible to discrete speech acts may be *immaterial* to the question of whether literary communication belongs to communicative action. That is, the reducibility of literary texts to discrete speech acts is not the main question in an account of literary communication as a form of communicative action. The main question is rather what validity claims are at stake in literature and literary discourse, and how these validity claims enable an intersubjective coordination of action. I will return to an argument for the notion of the extra-institutional coordination of action in the literary public sphere in 3.3.

   Sections 3.1.1.1–3 all shift the analytical focus from the individual speech act to a consideration of context: in 3.1.1.1, "considering the context" means taking an entire text (and/or its discussion) into account; in 3.1.1.2, "considering the context" means reconstructing the institutional conditions of that text's appearance (or the presuppositions in force in a particular exchange about that text); and in 3.1.1.3, "considering the context" means investigating the link between the literary institution and other social systems of action.

   Forbearing a demonstration of two of these components of communicative action (3.1.1.2 and 3.1.1.3) in the case of literature, it is already evident that Habermas's own elaboration of the concept of communicative action permits and in fact necessitates the extension of the concept to include certain uses of language other than standard forms of speech acts. On the basis of the three reasons mentioned above, it is apparent that it is not at all necessary to "break down" a literary text into discrete, component speech acts. The essential analytical operations are rather:

1. to distill the *validity claims* implicit and explicit in a literary text and its presentation and account for the raising and redemption of these validity claims (hence maintaining the other element in Habermas's explicit definition of communicative action as its (only) necessary condition);
2. to describe the background presuppositions involved in the various forms of discussion of literary texts (in accordance with 3.1.1.2 above);
3. to demonstrate the capacity of literary communication to coordinate action outside of the literary institution (in accordance with 3.1.1.3 above).

This approach allows one to evaluate literary culture in general as a *forum* of communicative action, and at least certain works and discussions in and on literary culture as *instances* of communicative action.

At this point I will indicate only that what connects the three aforementioned analytical aspects—the raising of validity claims through literary practice and discourse, the background presuppositions of the literary institution, and the action-coordinating capacity of literary culture—is the understanding of literature and literary discourse as made up of *performative* uses of language, by which I mean uses of language (not necessarily discrete speech acts), which are both *situative* and *intersubjective*.[6] Giving an account of the literary and literary-critical use of language as a form of communicative action *to the extent that it is performative,* has two important consequences:

1. Such an account *distinguishes* those literary and literary-critical uses of language from those uses not aimed at intersubjective communication.
2. It *correlates* the literary use of language with those *everyday uses* of language which consist of speech acts in this term's proper sense.

Although it is necessary neither to describe literary communication in terms of speech acts nor in terms of speech-act-analogous units of language use, one must understand the various manifestations of language use in literary culture as situated in the lifeworld context of everyday communicative praxis in order to see the literary public sphere as participating in the public sphere at large. In 3.3, I elaborate on the performative stance taken up by the various manifestations of language use in literary culture and give an account of the literary form of rationality under which they all operate. In the meantime I will address the revisions necessary in Habermas's *TCA* in order to understand aesthetic, and hence literary, rationality as a form of communicative rationality.

3.1.2 Theoretical Problems

3.1.2.1 *Aesthetic Rationality = Expressive Rationality*

Habermas incorrectly reduces aesthetic rationality to expressive rationality. He does this on the one hand by (1) categorically identifying aesthetic validity claims as truthfulness claims, and on the other hand by (2) characterizing modernization in the aesthetic realm as the fundamental concern with *innovation in expressivity*. This reduction results in an over-simplification of aesthetic rationality, insofar as aesthetic "argumentation," on Habermas's account, consists essentially in the demonstration of the genuineness of a particular self-representation. The claim most damning for aesthetic practice as a reasoning practice, however, is the argument, mentioned in the previous chapter, that aesthetic practice is rationalizable only as an expressive stance taken toward the objective and subjective worlds, but *fundamentally nonrationalizable* as a stance taken toward the social world. By *nonrationalizable* Habermas means parasitic on innovations from other (presumably theoretical and practical) value spheres. This view has serious consequences for the social relevance of aesthetic practice (and hence literature) in Habermas's theory of communicative reason. In this section, I argue against this view by showing that aesthetic rationality is irreducible to expressive rationality. My nonreductionist account holds not just that aesthetic rationality should not be reduced to mere expressive rationality, but rather that aesthetic rationality cannot be reduced to expressive rationality, as Habermas describes it, at all.

(1) Aesthetic Validity Claims = Truthfulness Claims

Truthfulness claims are different from truth or rightness claims to the extent that truth and rightness claims can be redeemed through arguments alone, Habermas argues, whereas truthfulness claims can only be "redeemed" through the observation of the consistency of a speaker's actions with his/her speech. This asymmetry leads to the first objection to Habermas's identification of aesthetic validity claims as truthfulness claims: we do not generally assume that the validity of a piece of literature, for instance, *as an aesthetic artifact*, relies on the consistency of its author's patterns of actions with it.

Habermas would counter this objection by qualifying the kind of truthfulness claim at work in the presentation of an aesthetic artifact: the claim of aesthetic validity is a claim of *authenticity*, to the extent that an aesthetic artifact is presented as constituting "an authentic expression of an exemplary experience."[7] The use of the attribute *exemplary* complicates

Habermas's classification of the authenticity claim as a form of the truthfulness claim, however. I will argue that it is right to describe the claim of authenticity as referring to an artwork's presentation of a complex of subjective experience that is *paradigmatic* (both representative and exemplary) for a shared experience, or at least *relevant to a shareable experience*. But Habermas does not go as far as giving such a definition. If he did, then he would not be able to classify the claim of authenticity as a kind of truthfulness claim, if what a truthfulness claim refers to is exclusively subjective experience. Authentic experience *as paradigmatic experience* necessarily refers to an intersubjectively shared (or shareable) experience, and hence does not satisfy the condition of referring solely to a realm of experience to which a subject has privileged access (which is Habermas's description of the truthfulness claim). This is the fundamental inconsistency in Habermas's account of the claim of aesthetic validity as a form of the truthfulness claim.

I argue that the authentic expression of experience is indeed both public and private, but not in the way that Habermas considers it to be. I hold that the claim of authenticity refers to the shared or shareable aspect of a subjective experience, i.e. to an individual self-representation that is held to accurately reflect a collective self-representation, whereas Habermas sees the authenticity claim as referring to *exclusively* private experiences that are nonetheless held to represent a shared experience. This contradiction in the nature of Habermas's account of the authentic expression of experience has consequences for the whole of his description of aesthetic rationality.

For one thing, it results in a problematic account of *aesthetic argumentation:* for Habermas, aesthetic argumentation consists, on the one hand, in an appraisal of the *authenticity* of a particular self-representation, and on the other hand, in an endorsement of certain *cultural value standards*. Habermas argues that aesthetic argumentation posits a relation of *justificatory priority* between these two elements: he wants to say that aesthetic argumentation seeks to endorse culturally specific value standards *by* explicating a self-representation as authentic. In aesthetic argumentation, he argues, the authenticity of a self-representation becomes the determining reason why one should accept particular value standards. But it is those particular value standards according to which the artwork is considered authentic in the first place. Given this state of affairs, Habermas asserts that aesthetic argumentation is a circular, and hence substandard form of argumentation, as I indicated in the previous chapter.[8]

Now, if the *truthfulness* claim were in fact always considered, ultimately, the determining criterion for the acceptability of the cultural value standards manifest in an artwork, then Habermas's conclusion would be right: clearly, the truthfulness of a self-representation does not alone warrant an acceptance (or rejection) of the value standards embodied by that self-representation.

But if one understands the claim of authenticity as referring to experience that is *paradigmatic* in a larger social context, then the argument for accepting a novel, for instance, as aesthetically valid, by no means relies solely on the *truthfulness* claim of its author as the determining reason for that acceptance. In his account of aesthetic argumentation, Habermas follows a correct intuition, i.e. he sees the necessity of distinguishing an *authenticity* claim from the *truthfulness* claim.

But Habermas simplifies the picture of aesthetic argumentation by nonetheless throwing authenticity and truthfulness claims into one conceptual bag: expressive rationality. He wants to show that in aesthetic argumentation the *authenticity* claim is taken as the legitimation of particular value standards. But, clearly, there are irreducibly *normative and descriptive aspects* to the claim of authenticity as the articulation of a paradigmatic experience. Both the (implicit or explicit) authenticity claim of an artwork and the (usually explicit) estimation of an artwork as authentic by a critic also, necessarily, raise claims about *objective* states of affairs and the *legitimacy* of a particular portrayal. The authenticity claim hence contains, in addition to a truthfulness claim, claims of *representation* in both senses of that word (*repräsentieren* and *vertreten*). Habermas is wrong to describe aesthetic argumentation only in terms of the upholding of particular, culturally specific value standards, when the authenticity claim, that he himself distinguishes from the truthfulness claim, contains irreducibly normative and descriptive elements. Because the authenticity claim is not reducible to the truthfulness claim, the aesthetic rationality that avails itself of the authenticity claim is not reducible to expressive rationality.

That truthfulness claims and claims of aesthetic validity are *not* coextensive is furthermore evident to the extent that aesthetic argumentation extends to include broader questions of lifestyle and taste, and not only the genuine articulation of subjective experience in art. This is so because the "expression" of a certain taste, through one's manner of dress, for instance, is not the same as the truthful representation of one's subjective world. That is, I can aesthetically evaluate someone's manner of dress without considering whether or not that manner of dress accurately reflects their subjective world (their preferences). And it is also not the case that my aesthetic appraisal of another's manner of dress necessarily reflects *only* my own subjective preferences. This is so because an aesthetic argument can appeal to *intersubjectively shared value standards*. This kind of value standards, the kind that are applied and criticized in aesthetic appraisals, are not always merely a product of subjective preferences. They are not normative in the way that ethical values are (i.e. attached to a claim of universal validity), but are shared to the extent that they reveal a general concern for the *stylization of human existence*.[9] The fact that the particular values concerning this stylization can and do vary between cultures and cultural groups says nothing against the universality of the interest itself. By bringing cultural value standards into his picture of aesthetic argumentation, Habermas thus himself suggests that aesthetic arguments need not refer to the truthfulness of self-representations at all. He would have to argue the contrary, however, if he wants to give an account of aesthetic rationality as reducible to expressive rationality.

Another inconsistency in his account of aesthetic rationality as expressive rationality is apparent in light of the universal status he originally attributed to the three forms of validity. On the one hand, Habermas argues that the three kinds of validity claims (truth, rightness, and truthfulness claims) are universal;[10] on the other hand, he holds that the kind of claim primarily at stake in aesthetic critique, the truthfulness claim, is not *strictly* universal.[11] Whereas cognitive and normative validity claims constitute universal validity claims in a strict sense, the validity claims deployed in aesthetic arguments presuppose a common store of values among recipients, but only among a specific group. Habermas argues that aesthetic *critique* by its nature validates culturally specific value standards, and hence is nonuniversalizable, whereas *discourses* (theoretical, practical, and explicative) are not culturally specific. But if aesthetic rationality were reducible to expressive rationality, it would only be able to give reasons for accepting the truthfulness of a particular (any particular) use of language. The goals of aesthetic critique lie elsewhere, however, as Habermas himself notes. But precisely because aesthetic critique does not aim only at an account of the conditions of acceptability of a truthfulness claim, the rationality operating through aesthetic critique is not reducible to expressive rationality. This particular inconsistency in Habermas's account of the universality of the truthfulness claim is a further indication that Habermas has not sufficiently thought through the distinctness of the authenticity claim from the truthfulness claim.[12]

(2) Modernization in the Aesthetic Realm as the Focus on Innovation in Expressivity

Another indication of Habermas's reduction of aesthetic rationality to expressive rationality is his attributing a central role to the augmentation, over time, of the value of *novelty in forms of expressivity* in the aesthetic realm: "With regard finally to value enhancement in the aesthetic domain, the idea of progress fades into that of renewal and rediscovery, an innovative revivification of authentic experiences."[13]

The cultivation of novelty does not consist primarily in the development of new artistic techniques, but rather in the aim at an ever "purer," more "genuine" expression of subjective experience:

> "Advances" in the domain of autonomous art move in the direction of an increasingly radical and pure—that is, purified of theoretical and moral admixtures—working out of basic aesthetic experiences. Avant-garde art achieved this value enhancement in part by way of becoming

reflective in its artistic techniques; the enhanced instrumental rationality of an art that makes its own production processes transparent enters here into the service of enhancing aesthetic value.[14]

Habermas's mentioning the avant-garde movements from the early twentieth century is intended to serve as support for his argument that *the predominant aim of aesthetic practice is expression,* a predominance won at the expense of descriptive and normative elements. The point of view from which the rationalization of the aesthetic sphere is possible is that of those abstract ideas that are, for Habermas, definitive for the autonomy of the expressive sphere of value: "beauty, authenticity, sincerity."[15]

The fact that Habermas mentions "authenticity" and "beauty" here makes his description of aesthetic practice as centered on the expression of merely subjective experience problematic. This is so because both *authenticity,* understood as presenting paradigmatic, shared experience, and *beauty,* understood as articulating certain shared value standards, indicate that aesthetic practice is also in the business of making normative claims. And even the mere use of "truthfulness" implies an irreducibly social aspect, to the extent that a truthfulness *claim* is validated, as Habermas himself argues, only through an *attribution* of truthfulness on the part of an audience, as I discuss below. This state of affairs would not present a problem, if Habermas were to give an account of the *intersubjective aspect of aesthetic value standards,* even if he maintains that art only *tends* to center on the expression of subjective experience. He does not give such an account, however. Indeed, he argues that aesthetic practice, as an expressive stance taken toward the social world, is *nonrationalizable.*

As mentioned in the previous chapter, Habermas makes this argument in his description of the possible (possibly rationalizable) combinations of the three formal concepts of the world (*formale Weltkonzepte*) with the expressive attitude (*expressive Einstellung*) toward the world:

1. the expressive attitude toward the *objective world* consists in *an aesthetic relation to one's nonobjectified environment;*
2. the expressive attitude toward the *social world* consists in *self-representation;*
3. the expressive attitude toward the *subjective world* consists in a *sensual-spontaneous relation toward oneself.*[16]

These expressive relations to the different "worlds" are exemplified, for Habermas, in:

1. artworks, style phenomena, and theories in which a morphological view of nature reigns;
2. social actions of the dramaturgical type;
3. affective utterances, libidinous stirrings, creative accomplishments, etc.

Habermas describes aesthetic rationality as including only the first and third groups of phenomena. In other words, aesthetic rationality is limited, for Habermas, to the expressive attitude toward the *subjective* world, which he cashes out in historical forms of *erotic practice*,[17] and to the expressive attitude to the *objective* world, which he cashes out in the form of *artistic practice*.

But it is not merely the case that art and erotic practice have historically embodied aesthetic rationality for Habermas, but rather that they are instances of *the only structurally rationalizable, expressive, formal-pragmatic actor-world relations*.[18] The expressive attitude toward inner nature (the subjective world) and outer nature (the objective world, but *not* the social world) constitutes "a complex of aesthetic-practical rationality, within which the production of knowledge can take the form of authentic interpretations of needs, interpretations that have to be renewed in each historically changed set of circumstances."[19] The focus of aesthetic rationality on subjective *needs* implies that Habermas considers the creation of art, for instance, *an expression of subjective needs*, and the (positive) critical interpretation of art as an *attribution of authenticity to an articulation of subjective needs*. But this focus on subjective needs does not preclude the possibility of considering the "self-representation" objectified by an artist in an artwork as a form of aesthetic rationality, as Habermas suggests. In fact, it is odd that Habermas seems to view the articulation of subjective needs before a real (listening) or virtual (reading) audience as not belonging to aesthetic rationality.

Now, Habermas does not make this exclusion explicitly, but the neatness of his tripartite architecture of (three) possible stances toward the (three) world(s) suggests it. What Habermas wants to call nonrationalizable in this context is *self-representation as dramaturgical action*. This consists in the predominant concern for the expressive function of language at the expense of its descriptive and normative functions, as discussed in more detail in the following section. For my argument, it is not at all necessary to argue against Habermas that the expressive stance toward the social world does consist, in fact, in a rationalizable set of practices. Rather, because Habermas reduces aesthetic rationality to expressive rationality, he suggests that there is no such thing as a rationalizable, *aesthetic* way of relating to the social world.[20] Once it has been shown, however that aesthetic practice is by no means captured by the representation of private (subjective) experience, but rather also raises truth and rightness claims, then one has at least eliminated the restriction of the domain of aesthetic rationality to the objective and subjective worlds. A description of how aesthetic rationality participates in a norm-regulated discourse (takes a rational stance toward the social world) would still have to follow. At this point, however, I want only to maintain that the domain of aesthetic rationality (the range of worlds toward which it, through the raising of validity claims, can take a rationally grounded stance) is by no means coextensive with the domain of expressive rationality.

I have just indicated that Habermas eliminates the expressive attitude toward the social world as a form of this aesthetic-practical rationality, because, he argues, it does not constitute a rationalizable formal-pragmatic relation to the world. It is interesting to see what example Habermas cites in order to support this claim of nonrationalizability:

> The fact that [the expressive attitude toward the social world does not take form], signals that expressively determined forms of interaction (for example, countercultural forms of life) do not form structures that are rationalizable in and of themselves, but are parasitic in that they remain dependent on innovations in the other spheres of value.[21]

Besides its being parasitic on other cultural spheres of value, Habermas gives no further argument for why he views self-representation a non-rationalizable practice, but a demonstration of the rightness or wrongness of his view in this regard is not relevant to my argument. This is so because the claim of aesthetic validity is not reducible to the claim of truthful self-representation, as shown in the previous section (3.1.2.1). For one thing, there is no reason to assume that the "countercultural lifestyles" that Habermas mentions primarily or necessarily foreground a truthfulness claim; these may just as well aim at the validation (or critique) of a normative claim. More important for my argument, however, is the fact that the example of countercultural lifestyles by no means captures what can be understood under an *aesthetic way of relating to the social world*. Literature represents, I will show, one such way of (rationally) relating to the social world (*as well as* to the objective and subjective worlds), and to this extent Habermas's delineation of aesthetic rationality is too narrow.

The restriction of aesthetic-practical rationality to the expressive attitude toward the objective and subjective worlds clearly has serious consequences for the social relevance of aesthetic (and hence, literary) practice in Habermas's theory of communicative reason. As mentioned in the previous chapter, however, even these practices of aesthetic rationality had negligible social import in Habermas's account:

> *Aesthetic-practical rationality* is institutionalized in the artistic enterprise. Of course, autonomous art has just as little structure-forming effect on society as a whole as do the shifting, unstable countercultures that form around this subsystem. On the other hand, the extraordinary values of this sphere form the focus for a hedonistic life-style directed toward innerworldly salvation, the life-style of the "sensualist" who is acting against the "pressure of the theoretical and practical" rationality of the ordinary "specialist," who is established in science, the economy, and the state.[22]

Habermas is willing to essentially relegate aesthetic-practical "rationality" to the private sphere, characterizing the engagement with art and counter-cultural forms of self-representation as an opportunity for escape from the functionalist reason of the everyday world. Aesthetic "rationality" is thus conceived as the practice of legitimizing a utopic retreat into the subjective world. This is one aspect of the social ignorance of aesthetic practice in Habermas's account: even the (rationalizable) expressive stances toward the objective world (engagement with artworks) and subjective world (cultivation of novel modes of self-representation) make no significant contribution to society.

The other aspect of this nonparticipation in the social world is the non-rationalizability of the expressive stance taken toward the social world mentioned above. The claim of the nonrationalizability of aesthetic practice *as* an expressive stance taken toward the social world that Habermas puts forth is relevant to my argument because of the narrow definition of aesthetic rationality that it offers. To clarify, I do not counter: (1) that the expressive stance toward the social world *is* rationalizable, and *therefore* (2) that aesthetic rationality includes more than Habermas claims. This is not enough because it presumes along with Habermas that aesthetic rationality is reducible to expressive rationality, which is untenable, as I argue above. I hold, rather, that *because* Habermas reduces aesthetic rationality to expressive rationality, he does not see the irreducibly intersubjective element in aesthetic practice; and it is for this reason that he misconstrues aesthetic rationality.

3.1.2.2 *Truthfulness Claim Bound to Concern for Perlocutionary Force*

As discussed in the previous section, Habermas identifies the claim of aesthetic validity as a form of the truthfulness claim. It is therefore relevant to his account of aesthetic rationality that he binds the raising and contestation of the truthfulness claim to a concern for the perlocutionary force of a use of language. Habermas's delineation of communicative action relies on the strict separation between the success-oriented and the communication-oriented uses of language, a separation which corresponds to a strict separation of perlocutionary effects from illocutionary content.[23] Perlocutionary effects are strictly excluded from the class of communicative actions. Given this exclusion and the strong connection between the aesthetic validity claim and a predominant concern for perlocutionary effects, Habermas clearly suggests that aesthetic practice does not belong to the class of communicative action. In this section I argue against this suggestion by showing the contingent nature of the connection of perlocutionary effects with the truthfulness claim. I do this by discussing two instances in Habermas's account of his connection of perlocutionary aim with the truthfulness claim: (1) Habermas's account of the relation between dramaturgical action and aesthetics forms of expression; and (2) Habermas's analysis of an example speech act. I also discuss Habermas's more recent formulation of the illocutionary/perlocutionary distinction.

(1) Dramaturgical Action and Aesthetic Forms of Expression

The connection of perlocutionary aim and the truthfulness claim is apparent in Habermas's exclusion of "dramaturgical" action from communicative action, as outlined in the previous chapter. The dramaturgical concept of action is paradigmatic for the utterance of propositions concerning subjective experience. Dramaturgical action, in itself, he argues, stresses the *expressive* capacity of language at the expense of the latter's descriptive and regulative capacities. Dramaturgical forms of action tend to presume only two worlds, the "performer's" (subjective) world and the objective world (which includes the "audience"). Furthermore, dramaturgical action tends to operate under the presupposition of an *opposition* between these two worlds. Because of the assumption of this opposition, dramaturgical action naturally tends to be strategic in nature: the "performer" makes utterances primarily with an eye to the effects that they will create among his/her audience. When a "performer" objectifies his audience in such a way, Habermas argues, he is operating in terms of strategic, and not communicative reason. Strategic dramaturgical action (any form of strategic action, for that matter) consists in the instrumentalization of illocutions for purposes external to them. Habermas does not argue that all dramaturgical action is strategic, but rather that dramaturgical action naturally tends toward the realization of perlocutionary goals. He furthermore identifies dramaturgical action with aesthetic forms of expression. The demonstration, however, of a dramaturgical action or pattern of dramaturgical action (a self-representation or pattern of self-representation) that aims at the realization of *illocutionary* goals, would provide a counter-example to the strong link between aesthetic practice and the predominant concern for perlocutionary effects, which, I will show, Habermas repeatedly suggests.

The dramaturgical concept of action does not qualify, in Habermas's account, as a form of communicative action. For this, the intersubjective medium of language and the coordinating effect of the raising and redemption of validity claims must supplement the dramaturgical concept of action. In the case of dramaturgical action, it is a claim of truthfulness that constitutes the illocutionary aspect: a contestable claim of truthfulness must be raised, at least implicitly, if the conditions of communicative action are to be satisfied. The raising of the truthfulness claim permits the contestation, Habermas argues, on the part of the audience, of the validity of the self-representation at hand.

An evident problem here is the *redeemability* of the truthfulness claim. Habermas wants to distinguish the truthfulness claim from the truth claim (to which it is nonetheless *analogous*), by showing that dramaturgical action is not reducible to the *description* of subjective experiences. Subjective experiences (wishes and feelings, for instance) are not (cannot be), he correctly argues, possessed in the way that objects are. Furthermore, neither the existence (nor nonexistence) nor the precise nature of particular subjective experiences are intersubjectively legitimizable or verifiable in the way that social norms or objective facts are. Particular subjective experiences are (socially) valid, Habermas argues, to the extent that they are articulated before an audience and are *attributed* to a subject by that audience.[24]

The aspect of this account of the distinctness of the truthfulness claims from the truth claim that is relevant to my argument are its implications for Habermas's earlier account of the redeemability of the truthfulness claim. According to that earlier account, truthfulness claims can only be redeemed through the observation of the consistency of a subject's actions with his/her speech acts. This means, however, that an *attribution* of truthfulness to an articulation of subjective experiences relies in part on an appraisal of truth conditions. That is, the truthfulness claim is parasitic on the truth claim, or, more exactly, the truthfulness claim is a special kind of truth claim. For me to accept as truthful John's statement "I love Mary," for instance, I have to observe certain, objectively verifiable patterns of behavior and furthermore reference social norms concerning was what counts as "loving someone." The details of an argument for the truthfulness claim as a form of the truth claim are not directly relevant here. What is directly relevant to my argument is the following: the fact that the truthfulness claim is parasitic on truth claims and often reliant on normative claims implies that the truthfulness claim can be fully redeemed only in the social context (i.e. a truthfulness claim is validated only through the *attribution* of truthfulness on the part of an audience).

Habermas himself describes the redemption of the truthfulness claim in this way, but does not draw the consequences of this account with regard to what might constitute a *communicative form of dramaturgical action*. The dramaturgical concept of action is, as Habermas uses it, an ideal type. That is, an action can be classified as dramaturgical and noncommunicative when it *tends to* foreground the expressive function of language without openly pursuing the illocutionary goals that it necessarily sets itself (the redemption of an at least implicitly raised truthfulness claim). Habermas does not claim that there is no communicative form of dramaturgical action (presumably, foregrounding the expressive function of language *while* openly pursuing one's illocutionary goals would, by contrast, constitute a communicative form of dramaturgical action). But Habermas does suggest that aesthetic forms of expression would not alone satisfy the conditions of a communicative form of dramaturgical action:

> The dramaturgical model of action presupposes language as a medium
> of self-presentation; the cognitive significance of the propositional

components and the interpersonal significance of the illocutionary components are thereby played down in favor of the expressive functions of speech acts. Language is assimilated to stylistic and aesthetic forms of expression.[25]

What Habermas says about the dramaturgical concept of action is most interesting here because of what it suggests about aesthetic forms of expression. His account of dramaturgical action has two related implications that are noteworthy in this regard: (1) aesthetic forms of expression are not per se communicative; and, more importantly, (2) aesthetic forms of expression per se focus on perlocutionary effects (to the extent that they downplay their own locutionary and illocutionary aspects).

(2) The Claim of Truthfulness and Perlocutionary Orientation

The strong link that Habermas suggests between truthfulness claims and the predominant concern for perlocutionary effects is especially apparent in his discussion of an example speech act.[26] The overall goal of his discussion of this speech act is to demonstrate that whereas speech acts generally foreground one validity claim, they can be criticized on the basis of all three, because every speech act simultaneously raises three (and only three) validity claims. The example that Habermas uses is a professor's request to a student during a seminar session to please bring him/her a glass of water. There are precisely three ways to criticize this speech act, Habermas argues: the addressed student (or any observer) can dispute (1) the normative correctness of the professor's request; (2) the truthfulness of the request; or (3) the truth of certain presumptions regarding objects and objective states of affairs. Objections of the first kind would consist in protestations of the sort: "No, you may not treat me like an employee of yours." Objections of the third kind would consist in protestations of the sort: "The nearest watertap is so far away that I would not be able to return to the seminar before the end of class." These protestations clearly reject the professor's speech act on the basis of its normative and objective presuppositions, respectively.

But is interesting to see how Habermas characterizes objections of the second kind, which demonstrate that the listener questions whether the speaker means (only) what he/she says. Habermas describes the second type of objection to the professor's speech act as one that consists in a protestation of the sort: "No, actually you just want to make me look bad in front of the other seminar participants." Here Habermas illustrates the rejection of a truthfulness claim with a case of *uncovering a perlocutionary aim*. Indeed, he makes this equation of the critique of truthfulness claims with a concern for perlocutionary effects explicit: "in the second [case], [what is contested is] that the professor means what he says (because he wants to achieve a certain perlocutionary effect)."[27]

The obvious question that arises at this point is whether the contestation of a truthfulness claim always also includes the alleged detection of a perlocutionary aim. Indeed, it does. The reason for contesting a truthfulness claim is that I object that a speaker *knowingly* does not say what she intends to bring about by saying what she does say. In Austin's terms, by contesting a truthfulness claim, I claim that the speaker wants to achieve a perlocutionary effect by means of her illocution. That is, she wants to get me, the listener, to react in a certain way to her utterance that is not specified by the utterance itself: the utterance is instrumentalized as a means to an end external to it. Such a strategic use of language works only if I, as the listener, do not recognize that there is an external purpose attached to the utterance and understand it only as an illocution, and thereby *attribute* truthfulness to the speaker. This attribution of truthfulness is an effect separate from whatever other external effects the speaker intends: it is an illocutionary effect, whereas what the speaker intends to achieve *by means* of the utterance is a perlocutionary effect.

I can also object that I do not believe what someone says without suggesting that he is attempting to produce a certain effect in his listener(s). This means that I hold that the speaker unintentionally says something other than what he means. But this does not constitute a rejection of the truthfulness claim. In such a case, I do not assert that the person is attempting to deceive (or indeed have *any* effect on) someone else, but rather that he is deceiving himself, to the extent that he does not correctly perceive, and hence does not clearly represent through his speech act, certain objective states of affairs, for instance. In this case I challenge the truth claims raised by the speaker, without necessarily doubting his truthfulness claim. One problem with Habermas's account is that the contestation of the truthfulness claim need not refer to subjective experiences. I can just as well object that someone is speaking untruthfully when I hold that they purposefully misrepresent *objective* states of affairs (and not just their own subjective experience), although I am *not* rejecting a truthfulness claim when I hold that they misperceive or unintentionally misrepresent objective states of affairs (this is another indication that the truthfulness claim is in some sense parasitic on the truth claim).

More important for my argument, however, is another problem with his account: whereas there is a conceptual connection between contesting a truthfulness claim and detecting a perlocutionary aim, there is no necessary connection between *raising* a truthfulness claim and having a perlocutionary aim. To raise a truthfulness claim is to appeal, implicitly or explicitly, to a listener or group of listeners to *attribute* truthfulness to one's utterance(s). Habermas correctly argues that the attribution of truthfulness is in general an illocutionary, and not a perlocutionary effect of a speech act (although a good strategic speaker will be able to create the mere impression of speaking truthfully). The truthfulness claim is, in his account, universal, in the sense that it is raised by virtue of the mere utterance of a proposition. I do not want to argue that Habermas holds that the *raising* of the truthfulness claim is per se attached to perlocutionary goals. The discussion of his example above is intended to show only that the *contestation* of a truthfulness claim is attached to an alleged detection of perlocutionary aims, in his account.

But Habermas is unclear on whether the relationship between the truthfulness claim and a concern for perlocutionary effects is an analytic or synthetic one. Indeed, his account is incomplete in general, as concerns the truthfulness claim: he explicitly establishes neither whether the *contestation* of the truthfulness claim is categorically coupled with a critique of perlocutionary aims, nor whether the *raising* of the truthfulness claim is categorically coupled with perlocutionary aims. Purely rhetorically, however, Habermas's illustration of the critique of the truthfulness claim leaves one thoroughly suspicious of the truthfulness claim in general. His account has this effect on the one hand due to his choice and analysis of examples, and on the other hand due to theoretical incompleteness in the respects mentioned above. This circumstance is significant for my argument because of its implications for aesthetic practice. Clearly, if the truthfulness claim is per se worthy of suspicion due to a predilection for perlocutionary goals, then so too is aesthetic practice an unlikely candidate for communicative agency, because it fundamentally relies on the truthfulness claim (or a form thereof).

(3) The Insufficiency of the Illocutionary-Perlocutionary Distinction

One concession that Habermas makes in his elaboration of communicative action should be mentioned at this point: Habermas concedes that perlocutionary effects can be *embedded in* a communicative use of language: strategic elements within a larger segment of speech can be distinguished from isolated perlocutions to the extent "that the entire sequence of a stretch of talk stands—on the part of all participants—under the presuppositions of communicative action."[28] This qualification *prima facie* contradicts Habermas's earlier, strict exclusion of perlocutions from the class of communicative actions. But in fact it represents a change in the level of analysis, from the individual speech act to the text (written or spoken). I hold that this is a productive shift in approach that Habermas unfortunately does not consistently follow through on. If Habermas is willing to accept perlocutionary elements within larger units of speech or text, *as long as* all parties involved operate under presuppositions of the communication-oriented use of language, then the characterization of communicative action that he provides in *TCA* is, if not one-sided, then at least incomplete.

He notes only the occasional need for indirect communication, which can be achieved through the realization of perlocutionary effects, effects that are pursued, however, with an eye to the *illocutionary* aspect of one's use of language. This suggestion remains vague with regard to how one is to evaluate the ultimate goal of a particular use of language. Specifically, if one cannot rely only on the individual speech act or even on the entire text in question, then one will have to move to a consideration of institutional presuppositions (or at least to a consideration of presuppositions in force in a particular exchange). Habermas takes the latter approach, but I argue that the former approach is just as valid. In the case of literature, for instance, a demonstration that the literary institution presupposes the communicative orientation of the perlocutionary aims of literature would qualify the "indirect" use of language in the literary realm as an at least potential form of communicative action. This is one possible way of revising the theory of communicative action to include literature. But this option has the disadvantage of selling literature short: namely, it suggests that literature fundamentally relies on perlocutionary effects. The account that I give suggests rather that Habermas's distinction between illocutionary and perlocutionary aims misses a vital aspect of the communicative potential of language: those effects which are neither specified in a particular illocution, nor are merely the effect of a strategic deployment of illocutions.

As indicated earlier, unlike Habermas, I distinguish between indirect uses of language and perlocutionary aims. There is a class of effects of language use which is indirect *and* nonstrategic, i.e. nonetheless communication-oriented. This proposed third class of effects is necessary to distinguish those observable effects of language that do not neatly fit Habermas's illocutionary/perlocutionary categorization. In his description of perlocutionary effects, Habermas accepts the criterion, proposed by Strawson, that *perlocutionary goals cannot be revealed,* if one wants to succeed. Illocutionary goals, on the other hand, are achieved *only if one pronounces them.*[29] I hold that what counts in evaluating literature as a form of communicative action is neither the (hidden) aim of the author nor the illocutionary content of a literary text itself, but rather, on the one hand, the *fact* that the literary artifact *is taken as* a communication-oriented act by an audience and criticized (valorized or rejected) on the basis of the claim of aesthetic validity read out of the text and its presentation; and on the other hand, the *redemption* of the claim of aesthetic validity that manifests itself in the public reception of a piece of literature. In subsequent parts of this chapter I will describe this aesthetic validity claim and what it is about aesthetically successful literary texts that makes literary culture a forum for communicative action. The effects that I am referring to are neither determinable on the basis of the text in question alone (illocutionary), nor are they dependent on any purpose which that text's author pursues (perlocutionary).

What does such a reclassification of the effects of uses of language give us, and how does this reclassification relate to the truthfulness claim, which begins the heading of this section? This section shows that truthfulness claims are not necessarily attached to a concern for perlocutionary effects; this in turn shows that aesthetic rationality is not necessarily attached to a concern for perlocutionary effects, because Habermas describes aesthetic rationality in terms of the raising and contestation of the truthfulness claim (or at least a form thereof). However, I do not follow Habermas's assumption that aesthetic rationality is concerned with truthfulness, in the first place, so why is it necessary to explicate the relation between the truthfulness claim and perlocutionary orientation at all? I do so for two reasons. First, in order to break down the deductive chain suggested by Habermas's account, according to which (1) aesthetic rationality is reducible to expressive rationality; which (2) consists in the raising and contestation of truthfulness claims; which in turn (3) demonstrate a dominant concern for perlocutionary effects; a concern which (4) constitutes a sufficient condition for being of form of strategic reason; hence leading to the conclusion that (5) aesthetic rationality is a form of strategic reason. Again, I do not claim that Habermas makes such a form of argumentation explicit, but rather that the architecture of his theory of communicative action permits and suggests it.

The second reason for analyzing the relation between the truthfulness claim and perlocutionary orientation is to give support to the proposed reclassification of the effects of uses of language, and show its importance in a consideration of literary rationality as a form of communicative reason. This reclassification is important because if I rely on Habermas's illocutionary/perlocutionary classification, then I either (1) restrict myself to classifying the effects of the literary use of language as the product of institutionally-sanctioned, and hence fundamentally communicative, realization of (nonetheless) primarily *perlocutionary aims;* or (2) I force myself to glean *illocutionary content* only from a text, which will be very messy at best, given the predominance of indirect strategies of communication in literature (through irony or satire, for instance). I will return to the aforementioned third kind of effect in my discussion of literary rationality as a unique form of aesthetic rationality, in order to support the view that the illocutionary content of a literary use of language is not fully internal to the literary text, but rather fundamental to the literary institution. The claim of aesthetic validity that is raised and contested in the literary institution is what makes up the illocutionary content of the literary use of language. It is literary rationality, which centers on this claim of aesthetic validity, that qualifies literary practice as a forum for communicative action. Seeking the illocutionary aspect of literature in texts alone leads to speculation; but giving up on the illocutionary force of literary language altogether falsely characterizes its role in the public sphere by denying its communicative rationality.

Habermas's more recent reformulation of the illocutionary/perlocutionary distinction also does not remedy the problems that I have indicated above. In "Handlungen, Sprechakte, sprachlich vermittelte Interaktionen und Lebenswelt"[30] Habermas introduces something like the further distinction among types of perlocutionary acts that I above argued is necessary in order to give an adequate account of the *communicative* effects of literary "speech acts." In this more recent article, Habermas distinguishes between perlocutionary$_1$, perlocutionary$_2$, and perlocutionary$_3$, which he delineates as follows:

perlocutionary 1: those effects that are internal to the speech act: the act of giving money to another after one accepts the request and hence obligates oneself to give money to another, for instance (in *TCA* Habermas called the giving of money part of the *il*locutionary success of the speech act).

perlocutionary 2: the nongrammatically regulated (i.e. external) consequences of the speech act, the nature of which is not implied *in* the illocution, but the success of which is *conditional upon* the success of the illocutionary aspect. The success of this kind of effect is not jeopardized when announced in advance, and hence qualifies as a "public perlocutionary effect." Habermas gives the example of the wife of the recipient of the money feeling happy when the promised money is given. The wife's feeling happy is not jeopardized by the announcement that this effect is intended with the giving of the money.

perlocutionary 3: the kind of effect that will not be achieved when announced in advance: a speaker wants to have the addressee give money to a third person for a purpose that the addressee would not condone. If the speaker announces his intentions he will not realize his perlocutionary goals (of the third or any other kind).

Although insightful, Habermas's further differentiation among types of perlocutionary effects does not get at the kind of communicative effects that I want to described as constitutive of literary rationality. This is so because Habermas still understands the truthfulness claim, with which aesthetic rationality primarily operates, as referring exclusively to the subjective experiences or *intentions* of the speaker.[31] Because he does not modify his account of aesthetic validity claims as referring to more than private experience, this more recent description limits the validity of a piece of literature to the attribution of truthfulness to the author on the part of her audience, or, alternately, to *the successful relay of the author's intention in presenting the work, through the work.* The communicative effects of literary practice that I am referring to are neither determinable on the basis of the text in question alone (illocutionary or perlocutionary$_1$), nor are they solely dependent on any purpose which that text's author pursues (perlocutionary$_2$ and/or perlocutionary$_3$). There is no convincing reason to believe that the communicative potential of a piece of literature relies exclusively or even primarily on the successful relay of the author's intention, although this aspect almost invariably *plays a role* in the aesthetic evaluation of a text. The aesthetically successful text *may* articulate its author's intention (or, alternately, *achieve* its author's goal if that text is latently strategic), but it always communicates *more than just the author's intention,* by virtue of the shared linguistic medium it avails itself of.

3.1.2.3   The Peculiarity of Literary Language as the Suspension of Illocutionary Force

Habermas is always quick to respond to his critics, and has done so in the case of criticism of his treatment of aesthetic rationality. In response to Wellmer's thesis of aesthetic validity as an interference phenomenon between all three dimensions of validity (which I later discuss in greater detail), and hence irreducible to expressive validity, Habermas reacts positively. He takes up Wellmer's suggestion of aesthetic coherence (*ästhetische Stimmigkeit*) as a distinct form of validity.[32] Habermas does not offer an account, however, of how this distinct form of validity relates to the three fundamental forms of truth, rightness, and truthfulness, or what consequences this new form of validity has for a revised understanding of aesthetic rationality. Aesthetic validity, for Habermas, essentially constitutes a unique form of validity precisely to the extent that it is not its own form of validity, as Seel correctly indicates.[33] Wellmer's suggestion is welcome, but Habermas is unable to actually accommodate it within the architecture of the theory of communicative action. Indicative of this is the fact that in the paragraph immediately following the last citation, and subsequently, Habermas again names expressive rationality and aesthetic rationality in one breath.[34]

The other significant aspect in Habermas's treatment of aesthetic rationality after *TCA* is his discussion of literature specifically, and the world-disclosing power of literary language. This treatment, similar to the inclusion of Wellmer's notion of aesthetic validity as aesthetic coherence, serves to reaffirm the suggestions with regard to aesthetic practice that were made in *TCA*, and does not offer a revised account of aesthetic rationality. Specifically, Habermas returns to Jakobson's definition of the poetic function as that aspect of a use of language which draws attention to the linguistic signifiers themselves. Habermas finds this description useful to the extent that it defines the unique character of literature. It is Habermas's aim in his essay on Derrida[35] to distinguish the literary from the philosophical use of language, in order to show how each mediates, in a different way, between expert cultures and the lifeworld. Whereas Derrida wants to see the priority of rhetoric to logic in all language use, and hence reads even philosophical works as works of literature, Habermas wants to show that literary criticism and philosophy constitute fully distinct forms of mediation: whereas literary criticism translates the experience manifest in literature into everyday language, philosophy relies on the "common sense" of everyday language, and focuses on the foundations of science, law, and morality. Whereas Habermas's delineation of the fundamental difference between philosophy and literary criticism has its valid and contestable points, the part of his account relevant to my argument is his characterization of the language of literature itself.

The Jakobsonian poetic function of language is what predominates in the literary use of language, in Habermas's account. That is, the *reflexivity of the literary signifier* is what is foregrounded in literature. For Habermas, literary language is unique in its linguistic creativeness and its world-disclosing capacity. Indeed, Habermas wants to raise literary language to the status of the *pure form of world-disclosure through language*.[36] But he does this with the help of a problematic assumption: that literary language is distinct in its *suspension of the illocutionary force of its own illocutionary acts*. Here Habermas relies on Richard Ohmann's definition of the literary: "A literary work is a discourse whose sentences lack the illocutionary forces that would normally attach to them. Its illocutionary force is mimetic." Specifically, a literary work purportedly imitates a series of speech acts, which in fact have no other existence. By so doing, it leads the reader to imagine a speaker, a situation, a set of ancillary events, and so on.[37]

The world-disclosing effect of literary language, for Habermas, relies on the deferment of illocutionary force, and hence also on a *suspension of the otherwise action-coordinating effect on illocutions*. Habermas again cites Ohmann: "Since the quasi-speech-acts of literature are not *carrying on the world's business*—describing, urging, contracting, etc.—the reader may well attend to them in a nonpragmatic way."[38] The described liberation from action-coordination and obligations that normally arise from the communication-oriented use of language is precisely what makes literary language the pure form of world-disclosure, for Habermas:

> The neutralization of the binding forces relieves the devitalized illocutionary acts of the pressure to decide in everyday communicative practice, displaces them from the sphere of ordinary speaking and thereby empowers them to playfully create new worlds—or rather: to demonstrate in pure form the world-disclosive strength of innovative linguistic expressions.[39]

It is interesting that Habermas chooses to characterize literary language in the way that he does, as eye-opening but noncommunicative, whereas literary *criticism* is described as serving a translation function: "The literature industry [as a cultural system of action] administers capacities of world-disclosure," i.e. translates the world-disclosure of literature into everyday language.[40] Because Habermas sees such a bridging function, it is odd that he does not consider the production of literature and literary criticism as belonging to one, literary, institution. How does he propose getting from the suspension of illocutionary force in literature itself to the communicative practice of literary criticism? I argue that the fact that illocutions within any literary text are not in force in no way implies that there is no illocution attached to the *presentation* of a literary text (its publication in any form). Central to Habermas's theory of communicative action is the idea that the *illocutionary role* should be conceived as that component that specifies *which* validity claim a speaker is raising with an utterance, *how* he/she is raising that claim, and *what* he/she is raising it *for*. In the case of literature, some of these specifications may (or may not) be available on the basis of the text alone. The full set of specifications, however, can only be observed with a consideration of the institutional context.

In another more recent article, in which Habermas himself tries his hand at literary criticism of a sort, the problems with Habermas's account of the peculiarity of the literary use of language becomes even more apparent. In his brilliant analysis[41] of Italo Calvino's *If on a Winter's Night a Traveler*, Habermas makes a convincing case against that author's attempt, through novel narrative techniques, to combine literature and literary theory by quite literally bringing the reader into the world of the novel. Habermas shows that despite Calvino's ingenious use of second-person forms of address directed at an ideal reader, the real reader always remains a distinct and autonomous rational entity in the act of reception, and is indeed *made into* a distinct dialogue partner by the author's engaging him or her in an almost literary-theoretical discussion. By addressing the reader directly and asking him to take a position on the validity claims *within* the text (to evaluate the speech acts of the novel's figures), however, Calvino unravels his own fictive merger of reader and text, Habermas argues. Habermas's point is, again, that the illocutionary force of speech acts within a literary text is suspended *for the author and reader:* a reader of a text cannot take a position with regard to a text-internal speech act in the same way that she can with regard to a speech act in the real world (presumably she can, however, take a position on the author's "speech act").

Here Habermas is quite close to arguing that the *author and reader* of a text at least potentially participate, through the production and reception of a literary text, in a communicative exchange with some sort of illocutionary force. But he doesn't go as far as this formulation. He says only that the speech acts of the figures in a literary text have no illocutionary force for the reader or author. When one sees the *presentation* of a literary text as raising, and the reception of a literary text as involved in the acceptance or contestation, of a complex claim of authenticity as described above, however, then literary communication clearly does have an illocutionary aspect in the nonliterary world. Habermas does not refute the existence of such a literary sort of illocution, but his account of the suspension of illocutionary force in text-*internal* speech acts does not leave much room for an understanding of literary practice as being very practice-oriented at all:

> In everyday communicative practice speech acts have a power that they lose in literary texts. In the former they function in contexts of action with which the participants deal with situations and—so be it—must solve problems; in the latter, they are tailored to a reception which relieves the reader of action: the situations which he encounters, the problems which he is confronted with, are not immediately his own.[42]

Habermas is quite right to point out, as he does in his analysis of Calvino's text, that the validity claims evident in speech acts within literary texts do not have the same status as validity claims in everyday speech: "The reader who takes a position toward the validity claims within the text as he would 'outside' in the everyday setting, reaches through the text for a thing—and destroys the fiction."[43] This state of affairs is in fact that which distinguishes literary texts from philosophical and scientific texts, on Habermas's account. Whereas in philosophical and scientific texts, Habermas argues, the reader is *supposed* to accept or challenge validity claims with regard to things or states of affairs in the world; aesthetic critique refers only to the process of world-disclosure.[44]

It bears repeating that whereas Habermas does not explicitly argue that literary language has no action-coordinating effects, his suggestion that literary language per se consists in the suspension of its own illocutionary force is misleading at best. I argue that Habermas's treatment of the literary use of language in particular, and aesthetic rationality in general, neglects and falsely characterizes a peculiar communicative potential that, according to the normative basis of his own theory of the public sphere, can, does, and *ought to* coordinate action outside of its immediate environment (the literary public sphere). In the following section I will prepare this argument by turning to alternative accounts of aesthetic validity and aesthetic rationality, in order to develop a new account of the interrelation of aesthetic validity with other forms of validity and that of aesthetic rationality with other forms of rationality. This is done with an eye to ultimately supporting the thesis that the literary use of language and the language of literary criticism, *when* it is communication-oriented, operates according to an aesthetic rationality that not merely *supplements* but is *a necessary component* of the reasoning practice of the well-functioning public sphere.

3.2   ALTERNATE ACCOUNTS OF AESTHETIC RATIONALITY

This section provides an account of recent work in aesthetic theory that considers itself a more or less direct answer to those aspects of Habermas's theory of communicative action that are relevant to aesthetic theory. It is important to note at the outset that the critiques and revisions of the theory of communicative action from the perspective of aesthetic theory are almost invariably and predominantly informed by Theodor Adorno's *Aesthetic Theory*,[45] which is widely understood as the single most important contemporary work on the topic. Whereas I cannot sufficiently treat Adorno's aesthetic theory itself in detail here, the latter's conceptual framework and normative thrust will be sufficiently illustrated by a description of those more recent contributions to aesthetic theory. In this section, it will become clear that the two central, related issues at stake in the interplay between aesthetic theory and the theory of communicative action are:

1. the status of aesthetic *validity* (and hence aesthetic validity *claims* and the *raising* and *redemption* of those claims) in relation to the three basic forms of validity propounded by Habermas (and their respective validity claims and the raising and redemption of those claims); and
2. the interrelation between different forms of *rationality,* including aesthetic rationality, under the umbrella concept of *reason.*

I contend that none of these critiques of the theory of communicative action alone presents an adequate and coherent account of the relation between aesthetic and nonaesthetic forms of validity on the one hand and between aesthetic rationality and nonaesthetic forms of rationality on the other hand, but use insights from all in order to present my own account of these relations (in 3.2.4).

3.2.1   Franz Koppe

Franz Koppe's *Fundamental Concepts of Aesthetics*[46] elaborates on Habermas's formal-pragmatic differentiation between (theoretical-cognitive) truth and truthfulness as component parts of the everyday conception of truth. Although he does not cite *TCA*, it becomes clear that Koppe's aesthetic theory understands itself as a development of Habermas's account of aesthetic rationality as expressive rationality, as I show here. Koppe distinguishes between *apophantic* truth, which corresponds to propositional truth in Habermas's theory, and *endeëtic* truth (from the Greek term signifying *needful*), which corresponds to expressive truthfulness in Habermas's theory.

Koppe underscores this distinction in part also in order to untangle Adorno's problematic notion of emphatic truth in art. Adorno had viewed truth in art as the only genuine form of truth, and hence as superior to everyday conceptions of (theoretical-cognitive) truth. Koppe, against Adorno, convincingly argues that it makes sense to posit a peculiar form of truth in art only when one can simultaneously describe what the nature of truth is, independent of its particular manifestation in art. Koppe argues, "It is reasonable to speak of the truth of art and its uniqueness in a theoretical context only when one also recognizes a theoretical truth claim distinct from it."[47]

Koppe's distinction between apophantic and endeëtic uses of language permits this conceptual independence of truth from the notion of truth in art: whereas apophantic speech makes assertions about the world that can be evaluated according to *objective* criteria, endeëtic speech, a peculiar form of which is the use of language embodied in art, articulates *subjective needs.*

Koppe focuses, above other art forms, on literature as the paradigm of his *signification-pragmatic* (*zeichenpragmatisch*) aesthetic theory. His demarcation of the endeëtic use of language as that use of language which articulates *subjective needs* indicates the *pragmatic* aspect of his aesthetic program. His focus on that use of *language* which articulates subjective needs renders Koppe's aesthetic theory a *theory of linguistic signification* (more specifically, a theory of *literary* signification). Hence the two halves of the attribute *signification-pragmatic.* Koppe understands his aesthetic theory as combining the dimensions required by an adequate aesthetic theory from the in themselves insufficient (1) *pragmatic* approaches to literary theory embodied in Marxist and psychoanalytic (literary) theory on the one hand, and (2) *theories of literary signification* represented by formalism and structuralism: "For the question *how* art is made as a sign of its own kind, cannot be reasonably separated from the question *why* it is thus made; and conversely, the question *why* it is so made cannot reasonably be separated from the question *how* it actually is made. What is sought after is thus a synthesis of both—for themselves weak in terms of the theory of art—in short, a *signification-pragmatic* aesthetics."[48]

Koppe thus correctly argues that an adequate aesthetic theory gives an account both of the *techniques* (the how) and the *motivation* (the why) of aesthetic practice.

Before providing his own account of the how and the why of aesthetic practice, Koppe catalogs criteria that have traditionally been held to determine the peculiarity of aesthetic signification, i.e. that which distinguishes it from all nonaesthetic forms of signification. *Innovation,* the reflexive *process* of aesthetic production and reception, the *indeterminacy* and *ambiguity, fictionality,* and *exemplarity* of its representations are all, according to Koppe, definitive elements of aesthetic systems of signification: all traditional aesthetic theories postulate (at least one of) these criteria as necessary conditions for qualifying as an aesthetic artifact or practice. But none of these criteria nor any combination of them, Koppe argues, sufficiently allows for an account of the *specificity* of aesthetic signification, because they do not describe *what* is communicated through art.[49] Each of these criteria is sufficiently fulfilled in other realms of practice,[50] and aesthetic theories that do not specify *with regard to what* a practice is innovative, indeterminate, exemplary, etc., therefore do not give an account of the particularity of aesthetic practice at all, he argues.

In contrast to those aesthetic theories that identify a cognitive or normative content in aesthetic signification, such as ones that deploy the above criteria, an aesthetic theory that avails itself of an *emotive* theory of meaning sees the essential function of art in its production of feelings, i.e. only perlocutionary effects, in the recipient. Koppe argues that this emotive aesthetics (*Gefühlsästhetik*) likewise does not adequately describe the specificity of aesthetic signification, because meaning is never fully reducible to feeling. Koppe, against emotive aesthetic theory, wants to make a case for the *communicative* ability of aesthetic practice: "Meanings are even not identical with emotions when, as the case may be, emotions are meant. [...] The psychologization of the theory of art does not do justice to the symbolic character of art, because it misses the latter's character of communicative action—in both production and reception."[51]

And in contradistinction to the *partial* accounts of the communicative character of aesthetic practice provided by the criteria mentioned in the previous paragraph, Koppe asserts that the *specificity* of aesthetic practice lies in its (superior) ability to articulate human needs, to express concernment (*Betroffenheit*), i.e. "[the] *change in one's own situation of need* [...] also and not lastly with regard to the situation of need of others."[52] This is the *what* of literary signification, in Koppe's account.

The *how* lies, according to Koppe, in the *connotative* capacity of literary language.[53] It is the connotative capacity of literary language that makes it for Koppe superior in the aforementioned regard, i.e. in the *public* articulation of human situations of need: "Literature, as institution of aesthetic speech, aims—seen as a whole—decidedly to make silent concernment, closed-off experiences of need, public, beyond the capacities and the horizon of common speech in a linguistically creative manner."[54]

The unusual semantic richness of poetic language enables, by virtue of the shared linguistic medium, the intersubjective visualization of a situation as a situation of need, Koppe argues. Superior to nonaesthetic speech due its *connotative* capacity, aesthetic, i.e. poetic speech is distinct to the extent that it *tacitly* articulates situations as situations of need, precisely because it does so through *con*notation, not denotation.

But Koppe is intent on showing not just that aesthetic speech is one distinct way among other ways of articulating human needs, and likewise not just that it is a purportedly superior way of articulating needs, but rather also that moral discourse, for instance, which aims in part at the *explication* of human needs, must at least sometimes rely on the *implicit* articulation of these through aesthetic speech. Koppe argues for the occasional *necessity* of poetic language to Habermas's consensus-oriented model of public communication, citing Habermas's own description of the peculiar "poetic ability to interpret the world in light of human needs."[55] The value of the aesthetic use of language for a theory of communication thus lies for Koppe in its potential to articulate human needs in such a way that strictly descriptive or normative modes of communication cannot. Koppe cites Habermas's argument that moral argumentation must indeed sometimes rely on this potential of aesthetic practice:

> As soon as we propose a new interpretation of needs, a different light falls on that which the discourse participants believe to want in a given situation. A reinterpretation of conventions of need can be the result of a self-reflection which makes one's own inner nature transparent and corrects self-delusion; it can also be the result of a creative process of

semantization which unleashes potential for new meanings via the non-propositional symbolic systems of literature, art and music. To this extent, moral argumentation relies on the, be it therapeutic or artistic-creative, elimination of barriers to communication.[56]

Koppe interprets Habermas's concession to artistic practice as attributing it the character of a creative *eros*, to the extent that its aim is the overcoming of the barriers of the everyday articulation of needs and the communicative exchange between human subjects *as needful entities*. In addition to this "erotic" element, Koppe postulates a "utopic" element as constitutive of the specific nature of aesthetic valuation.[57]

Whatever Habermas's response to such an account of the role of artistic practice and aesthetic critique in communicative reason would be, at least the following accord between Habermas and Koppe can be established: to the extent that Habermas holds (1) that any consensus on values and norms cannot be blind to human needs; and (2) that aesthetic practice possesses a peculiar capacity to create new meanings *in light of situations of need,* he would agree with Koppe's argument that moral discourse, at least sometimes, relies, even must rely, on poetic language.

While Koppe rightly indicates the interrelation between aesthetic practice and normative discourse in Habermas's own theory, there are two other aspects to his (Koppe's) characterization of the literary use of language that make his account of aesthetic rationality's contribution to communicative reason problematic. Koppe summarizes his definition of the aesthetic use of language as follows: "Aesthetic speech is overbidding endeëtic speech. And it is overbidding, namely, compared with practical speech: in particularly connotative ways, with its phenomenal contingency suspended, in counterfactual correspondence with the need for contingency-suspending meaning of life."[58] The two aspects that I want to focus on briefly here are (1) that the connotative process of literary language includes a reflexive reference to the phenomenality of its own character as a systems of signifiers, a reference that aims, through "aesthetic form," at annulling the *contingency* of this phenomenality; and (2) that the literary use of language fulfills the "fundamental human need for contingency-suspending meaning of life, a need that it counterfactually evokes as satisfied in its 'form'."[59] These two related features of the aesthetic use of language in Koppe's account need some explication.

Koppe wants to show that "aesthetic form," the form of a poem for instance, necessarily evokes a sense of wholeness, even when what is portrayed within that aesthetic form is an experience of the most irrevocable fragmentation and deepest alienation. For this purpose, Koppe compares "Septembermorgen," a poem by Eduard Mörike that evokes the beauty of nature, and "Sturmangriff," an Expressionist poem that depicts the horror of the trenches in World War I. I cannot elaborate on the analysis of this unseeming pair of poems here. What is important is Koppe's claim that the text of the Expressionist poem, despite the traumatized experience that it portrays, and despite the fragmentation of syntactic units through which it does this, nonetheless, *counterfactually,* evokes a whole, through its articulation of a situation as a situation of need, here, indeed, as a situation of desperation. This it does, Koppe argues, by virtue of its *purposeful presentation* of the fragmentation of human experience. This purposeful presentation of fragmentation refers necessarily to the whole that has been lost and/or which is envisioned, he argues. The Mörike poem also evokes a whole through its articulation of a situation as a situation of need, but here the situation is one of *fulfilled* subjective need. "Septembermorgen" is not, Koppe argues, a mere description of a September morning as an event *in* the objective world from the perspective of a subject that is also *in* the objective world, but rather, through its connotative use of language, evokes the (fulfilled) *experience* of that morning as a situation in which the subjective world of the poetic "I" *is* the world. Thus, here too the poetic "I" aims at nullifying contingency, by presenting its situated and transitory experience of the world *as* the world.

What the two poems, seeming opposites, have in common, Koppe argues, is their attempt to overcome, through the connotative use of language, the phenomenality of both *what* they portray and *the means through which* they portray what they portray. Poetic texts, Koppe argues, portray the contingency of human life and reflexively portray the phenomenality of their own signifiers. That is, whether the aesthetically presented experiences are those of fulfilled or unfulfilled need, the poetic use of language aims at nullifying both the contingency of human life and the contingency of the system of linguistic signification of which it avails itself. Through its aesthetic form, i.e. its phenomenal appearance as a distinct unity, and its aesthetic means, i.e. its richly connotative use of language, a poetic text aims at, counterfactually, *nullifying* contingency and phenomenality in each these respects.

By this point it is clear that Koppe's definition of the peculiarity of speech art turns on the functional link between (1) the reflexive reference of poetic language to (and the attendant attempt to counterfactually nullify) its own phenomenality; and (2) its reference to (and the attendant attempt to counterfactually nullify) the contingency of human life. Here I want to argue neither against this connection in particular nor against the particular anthropological presuppositions that are made in Koppe's argument. I do want to point out, however, that the intention of counterfactually nullifying the contingency of human life *does not follow from* the circumstance that the literary use of language is particularly well adapted to (tacitly) articulating situations of human need, as Koppe's argument suggests. Furthermore, one can identify the *peculiarity* of the literary use of language with respect to the articulation of human needs without also asserting its *superiority* in this regard, as Koppe does.

One can rather, as I want to, see the peculiarity of literary language not as its being a purportedly superior mode of articulating subjective experience, but rather as consisting in its capacity to articulate *ways of looking at* the objective, social, and subjective worlds *in light of* shareable subjective experiences. This formulation loosens up an odd restriction in Koppe's argument: on the one hand he adheres to Habermas's reduction of aesthetic practice to the expression of subjective experience; on the other hand he insists on the communicative character of this expression. The problem with Koppe's account is not this part of the description alone, but rather that it assumes a *particular* bridge between the aesthetic articulation of any given complex of subjective experience and other subjects: the need for a contingency-nullifying sense of life. This allegedly essential human need does all the work in Koppe's argument that aesthetic practice articulates *shareable* experience. One does not have to argue against this particular anthropological presupposition when one argues against this being the *exclusive or primary* function of the literary use of language: I merely want to argue that there are a host of other needs that can be presented by means of aesthetic artifacts. Koppe's own indication, mentioned above, that the *connotative richness* of poetic language enables the intersubjective visualization of situations as situations of need, suggests that there is no particular restriction on *what kinds* of situations of need are thus articulated.

There is another aspect of Koppe's account of aesthetic practice that reflects the above mentioned problem of the communicative character of aesthetic forms of subjective expression: the ambiguous definition of aesthetic *coherence*. The aesthetic *coherence* of a poetic text is not a function, Koppe argues, of the harmony of (1) the *contingency* of human life portrayed in that text with (2) the *form and linguistic means* through which the text aims at annulling this contingency. Indeed, these often enough oppose one another. Aesthetic *coherence* is rather a function of the *fit* of parts to a respective whole:

> Aesthetic *coherence* of a text is, put more precisely, the fit which reaches into its phenomenality, of the parts to the whole. As endeëtic coherence it does not, admittedly need to be harmonious at all, because endeëtic 'contradictions' (unlike apophantic ones) do not exclude one another—as little as in life. In particular, therefore, that dialectic between the represented contingency of life and its contingency-overcoming form of representation, a form which may even represent its mirror image, without losing aesthetic coherence, even with a gain in its connotative density and reach, is possible.[60]

As Koppe uses the term here, *Stimmigkeit* could be translated as *coherence,* designating, in particular, the good fit of the component parts to the whole of the aesthetic artifact. But this is only one, formalist sense of *stimmig* as it is used here: on the one hand Koppe is talking about the well-formedness of the aesthetic artifact as a self-sufficient construction. On the other hand, *stimmig* refers here to resonance *in an audience*. This sense is, of course, also central to Koppe's understanding of aesthetic practice as a *communicative practice*.

The centrality of this second sense of aesthetic resonance in Koppe's aesthetic theory is evident in his account of "truth in art." Koppe addresses the question of truth in art in terms of the public nature of the institution of literature, and the *paradigmatic* nature of its artifacts. "Truth" in literature does not, for Koppe, have to do merely with the truthfulness claim of individuals, nor does the literary use of language itself raise a truth claim that is analogous, in a straightforward manner, to a proposition. In claiming to present an experience of need in both an *exemplary* and *representative* way (exemplary to the extent that a *general* experience is embodied in a concrete example, and representative to the extent that a *group-specific* experience is presented, together *paradigmatic*) the literary use of language raises an *adequacy claim*, Koppe argues. That is, a piece of literature claims to embody a fitting example. This adequacy claim is by no means reducible to a truth claim, which posits a perfect reflection or description of objective facts or states of affairs. This is why, for Koppe, aesthetic speech (and the literary use of language as a form thereof) is not translatable into apophantic (assertory) speech.

But the legitimate adequacy claim also does not alone provide a sufficient description of truth in art, for Koppe. Any particular adequacy claim does not fully capture the peculiarity of aesthetic speech, Koppe argues, because any particular complex of subjective experience presented in or through an aesthetic artifact cannot be completely subsumed under the shared experience for which it is taken to be paradigmatic. In other words, there is always a purely subjective remainder, even in the most paradigmatic representation, or, more exactly, the *situatedness* of the author is never fully captured in the paradigmatic situation that she articulates through her aesthetic practice. Furthermore, to fully qualify as an aesthetic use of language, Koppe argues, the must be no endeëtic contradiction between "situation" and "dream," i.e. no *false harmonization* of reality and vision. As examples of quasi-aesthetic uses of language that falsely harmonize reality and vision, Koppe names the language of advertising in contemporary media society on the one hand, and trivial literature on the other hand.

Given the above restrictions, Koppe considers the truth claim of a particular literary art to be validated when that artwork (1) is subjectively truthful; (2) is paradigmatic (adequately depicts a shared complex of experience); and (3) does not falsely harmonize vision and reality. No one of these one of these conditions is alone sufficient to qualify a work of literary art as aesthetically valid, on Koppe's account: only the satisfaction of all three validates the claim of aesthetic "truth." Given the third restriction, however, it is not clear how Koppe proposes to distinguish between the deficient forms of the aesthetic use of language mentioned in the previous paragraph and certain other forms which he certainly considers aesthetically valid, such as Romantic literature, which also does not satisfy the third condition. Koppe draws a qualitative distinction in this regard only to the extent that he distinguishes aesthetic "truth" in the broad sense and aesthetic "truth" in the narrower sense. Koppe summarizes his account of truth in art thus:

> Aesthetic speech is (in the broader sense) true, when it is endeëtically truthful and [...] paradigmatically accurate; it is (in the narrower sense) aesthetically true, when it, in so doing, does justice to its endeëtic character of overbidding without falsification, which means: without describing unfulfilled or unfulfillable needs as fulfilled or fulifillable in real life.[61]

The unfulfilled and unfulfillable needs of which Koppe speaks here are apparently reducible to the essential human need for a contingency-nullifying sense of life that he had identified earlier as motivating all genuinely aesthetic speech. How will this thesis of the *absence of false harmonizations* in aesthetic speech square with the *counterfactual nullification of the contingency of human life* that he sees as equally constitutive of aesthetic speech? Presumably Koppe will have to rely on something like Romantic irony in order to make these two aspects cohere. He does not make this move, however, and also does not explain how these two can cohere in non-Romantic forms of literature.

It is furthermore not clear in what sense Koppe requires aesthetically "true" literature to be subjectively truthful from the perspective of the author (the first condition of aesthetic "truth" mentioned above). Naming Flaubert as an example, Koppe suggests the necessity of a correspondence between an author's own biography and the life story of his protagonists. This actually constitutes a truth claim, however, and not a truthfulness claim. And it is not at all self-evident that such a truth claim is part of the claim of aesthetic validity. It seems rather to be the case that the fictional, paradigmatic representations in literature raise validity claims not with regard to a purportedly *objective* reflection of lived experience, but rather raise claims with regard to the objective and social worlds *in light of* lived experience. I will ultimately illustrate this point in my literary analysis in Chapter 4. Such an understanding of the aesthetic validity claim eliminates the requirement of a legitimate truthfulness claim for aesthetic validity (when truthfulness is understood in this autobiographical sense).

What is valuable in Koppe's aesthetic theory for my argument is the thesis that the articulation of subjective needs in and through aesthetic artifacts is inherently intersubjective and hence belongs to communicative reason. Aesthetic practice is intersubjective not because it articulates any *particular,* allegedly shared need, as Koppe suggests, but rather to the extent that that it claims to present any paradigmatic experience at all. The status of this claim is always rationally contestable, but this is a practice of reason that is fully reducible neither to (1) the contestation of a truth claim nor to (2) the contestation of a truthfulness claim. Koppe is clear on the first of these aspects: the relation between propositional truth and "truth" in art is for Koppe at most one of complementarity and mutual irreducibility. Aesthetic truth does not trump propositional truth, as Heidegger or Adorno would have had it, Koppe argues; and theoretical truth cannot explain away aesthetic truth, as Hegel would have had it. "Speaking art is [...] not at all a genuine *site of truth* [...]. Rather, it is, precisely because art in this (apophantic) sense does not need to be the site of truth, the communicatively superior *site of concernment*—as the case may be, *through* truth."[62]

Koppe's aesthetic theory rightly reformulates the traditional understanding of art as an enhanced expression of subjectivity into a theory of aesthetic communication that neither privileges art's status in relation to truth nor relegates art to the realm of the irrational, i.e. releases art from the constraints of rationality.

But Koppe is less clear on the second of the above-mentioned aspects, the irreducibility of the claim of aesthetic validity to expressive truthfulness: on the one hand he sees the aesthetically valid artwork as paradigmatic; on the other hand he sees aesthetically successful communication as validating a claim of subjective truthfulness on the part of the author, and hence as embodying an *expressive rationality*. This is evident in his concentration on *concernment*. To be sure, Koppe acknowledges the constitutive role of the perceived needs of others in the aesthetic articulation of a change in one's own situation of need. But in the final analysis, making *concernment* the defining characteristic of the aesthetic use of language renders aesthetic practice, on both its productive and receptive sides (writer and reader/listener) a practice of uncovering fundamentally *subjective* experience: "[the] change *in one's own* situation of need [...] also and not lastly with a view to the situation of need of others."[63] In this, Koppe, despite his insistence on the communicative character of aesthetic practice, follows Habermas's reduction of aesthetic rationality to expressive rationality.

I have already argued that it is not at all necessary to assert the *superiority* of aesthetic practice in expressing and recognizing situations as situations of need, as Koppe does. In a sense, Koppe does this precisely because he sees the aesthetic use of language as a richer form of everyday statements of subjective experience (*Erlebnissätze*). Once one no longer restricts the domain of aesthetic rationality to the expression of subjective experience, however, it is no longer necessary to assert a superiority of aesthetic language in order to define its peculiarity. I indicated above that understanding aesthetic validity claims as containing subsidiary validity claims of all the types that Habermas identifies lets one see the peculiarity of literary language as consisting in its capacity to articulate *ways of looking at* the objective, social, and subjective worlds *in light of* shareable subjective experiences. Koppe's account doesn't allow for this possibility because it makes aesthetic rationality into an expressive rationality that avails itself of truthfulness and truth claims. The *normative* claim, for instance, which necessarily inheres in the claim of paradigmatic representation, receives no attention at all in Koppe's account. The interrelation between the three fundamental forms of validity is constitutive of the aesthetic validity claim, and I now turn to an account which makes this interdependence central to his theory of aesthetic validity.

3.2.2   Albrecht Wellmer

Albrecht Wellmer's reception of Habermas is more critical than Koppe's as concerns those aspects of Habermas's theory of communicative action relevant to aesthetic theory. Wellmer's critique is clearly delineated in his talk at the 1983 Adorno Conference in Frankfurt.[64] Wellmer's talk on Adorno's aesthetic theory is of interest to my argument because it specifically addresses the question, mentioned at the beginning of this section, of the independent status of aesthetic validity and aesthetic validity claims with regard to other forms of validity. Wellmer begins by referring to Adorno's earlier collaboration with Max Horkheimer, *Dialectic of Enlightenment,* as a key text for understanding the posthumously published *Aesthetic Theory.*[65] A dialectic of subjectification (*Subjektvierung*) and objectification (*Verdinglichung*) is developed in *DoE,* and a dialectic of aesthetic appearance (*Schein*), is alluded to there as well. Wellmer sees the interpenetration of these two dialectics as the central principle of the much later *AT.*[66] He furthermore describes *DoE* as an attempt to bring together the two disparate philosophical traditions represented by (1) the critique of reason, from Schopenhauer, to Nietzsche, to Klages; and (2) the critique of political economy from Hegel, to Marx, to Weber, to Lukacs. In *DoE,* Wellmer writes, the process of civilization as the "self-emancipation" of humanity from nature on the one hand (1), and class domination in society on the other hand (2), are viewed as complementary steps in the dialectic of subjectification and objectification. The process of civilization is described by Adorno and Horkheimer as the coming to dominance of instrumental reason. The instrumental mind, itself a product of living nature, comes to conceive itself only in terms of *dead* nature; it objectifies itself. The process of civilization is for Adorno and Horkheimer a process of the self-alienation of the instrumental mind.

As good Hegelians, however, Adorno and Horkheimer see the process of civilization simultaneously as a process of enlightenment. The concepts of reconciliation, happiness, and emancipation can be considered solely as products of enlightenment thinking for them. And enlightenment, so the argument goes, can only be surpassed and perfect itself through its own medium, instrumental reason. Hence enlightenment must enlighten itself by countering through reason the negative results of its use of reason. Wellmer paraphrases the ambivalent cultural critique of *DoE* thus: "The enlightenment of the Enlightenment over itself, the 'remembrance of Nature in the subject' is only possible in the medium of the concept; the precondition is, certainly, that the concept turns against the objectifying tendency of conceptual thinking."[67]

Elsewhere Adorno describes such self-critique as the defining feature of philosophy as such: "Through it [philosophy] the endeavor is to go beyond the concept by means of the concept."[68]

This self-surpassing of philosophy is seen by Adorno as the joining of rationality with what he designates the "mimetic" moment. Here is where art enters the picture. *Mimesis,* as "the sensually receptive, expressive and communicatively nestling behaviors of the living" is found in paradigmatic form in art: art is "mimesis, sublimated, i.e. transformed through rationality and objectified."[69] The mimetic moment of art enables the rational mind to break through its own self-inflicted objectification. Adorno hence posits the mutual necessity of art and philosophy. The utopic motivation of both art and philosophy, on Adorno's account, is reconciliation, the reconciliation, more specifically, through mimesis, of the self-objectified mind with the nature concealed within it. *Instrumental reason* designates a structuring principle in the relations between humans and between humanity and nature, an artifice violently imposed on the living. *Reconciliation* hence and by contrast represents for Adorno the "nonviolent unity of the much in a reconciled connection with all that is living."[70] Art and philosophy provide a model for this unity, the unity of perception and concept (*Anschauung und Begriff*), of particular and general, of part and whole. By virtue of their utopic dimension, both art and philosophy relate antithetically to the world.[71]

On the other hand, however, philosophy and art also stand in an antithetical relation to one another: discursive and nondiscursive knowledge, philosophy and art, respectively, both want to embody the totality of knowledge, but each grasps only a portion of truth; for the "whole truth" to be there, reality itself would have to be reconciled. In the artwork, Adorno asserts, truth *appears;* in this lies its priority over discursive knowledge (philosophy). But because it merely *appears* to the senses, the truth in art simultaneously veils itself. Adorno compares the artwork to puzzles and picture puzzles (*Vexierbilder*), something which appears and in appearing hides itself from perception.[72] And this is where philosophy comes into the picture: art must be interpreted, its truth content articulated through philosophical interpretation: "Genuine aesthetic experience must become philosophy, otherwise it *is* not at all [my emphasis]."[73] Yet philosophy cannot fully restitute the truth content of art. Together art and philosophy can only circumscribe a truth that neither of them can utter. The "language" of art (and for Adorno this is primarily the "language" of music) and language proper exist as separate halves of an ultimately inaccessible "true language."[74]

The truth content of art, in Wellmer's account of Adorno, is not merely a matter of propositional truth, but rather a function of (1) its reference to the beauty of *nature* and (2) its utopic representation of a *reconciliation* with nature: "Art does not imitate the real, rather, at best, that of nature which points beyond reality: the naturally beautiful"; reconciliation with nature is "a fetterless together of the much that is not aggrieved in its peculiarity."[75] Whereas the relation between art and philosophy is for Adorno, as described above, *aporetic* (a relation of two incomplete, mutually complementary parts of a whole, "true language"), the relation between truth, reconciliation, and aesthetic appearance (*Schein*) is *antinomous*. This is what Wellmer designates the dialectic of aesthetic appearance.[76] The antinomy consists in (1) the fact that art is true only insofar at it represents reality as it is, i.e. unreconciled; but (2) it can only do this through an aesthetic synthesis that presents an appearance of reconciliation:

> It [art] can only be true in the sense of faithful to reality to the extent that it brings it [reality] to appearance *as* unreconciled, antagonistic, tattered. But it can only do that by making reality appear in the light of reconciliation, through nonviolent aesthetic synthesis of the abstracted, which generates the aesthetic appearance of reconciliation.[77]

Wellmer is careful to separate two meanings of true that Adorno does not distinguish in the above analysis: (1) true in the sense of *aesthetic coherence* (*ästhetische Stimmigkeit*); and (2) true in the sense of objectively valid. What Adorno, in end effect, wants to say, Wellmer argues, is that art can represent knowledge of reality (truth in sense 2) only when it coheres aesthetically (is true in sense 1); and that art can resonate aesthetically (sense 1) only through an accurate representation of reality (sense 2). The *antinomy* of aesthetic appearance consists in the fact that art must simultaneously *instantiate* and *resist* its own founding principle (aesthetic appearance, i.e. mere *Schein*), for truth's sake.

Wellmer describes Adorno's account of aesthetic experience with modifiers such as "distant from reality," "ecstatic," and "not real-utopian."[78] But he also describes Adorno's philosophy as standing on a "fault line between historical materialism and utopian sensualism."[79] With this evaluation of *AT*, Wellmer argues there are materialist elements to Adorno's idealist aesthetic theory that are, despite its idealism, salvageable for a theory of aesthetic communication. Herein lies the connection to Habermas's theory of communicative action, because this kind of critique of Adorno is precisely the kind that Habermas undertakes in the second half of Chapter 4 of *TCA*.

On Habermas's account, Adorno is still in the service of the philosophy of consciousness (*Bewußtseinsphilosophie*): the structural asymmetry of the subject–object relation in Adorno leaves no room for an intersubjective, i.e. communicative moment. Habermas locates this communicative moment in the world-disclosing function of (everyday) language (*welterschließende Funktion der Sprache*). The place held by language in Habermas is held by *mimesis* in Adorno: on Adorno's subject-object model of the world the "communicative" moment, in order to not constitute merely another instantiation of instrumental reason, must lie *external* to the realm of conceptual thinking. Because Adorno sees discursive reason as inherently instrumental and does not have a theory of intersubjectivity, he can give an account of "communication" only in terms of *mimesis,* through which the subject can at best recover layers of meaning buried within *itself.* Whereas Adorno sees in the practice of reason only instrumental rationality, Habermas argues for communicative reason, to which instrumental rationality is subordinate, or at least can be subordinated.[80] Whereas Adorno sees the mimetic moment that counteracts instrumental reason in its paradigmatic form in art, Habermas sees a *mimetic moment in everyday language.*

Once the dialectic of subjectification and objectification has been dissolved, as Habermas suggests in *TCA,* however, the question remains as to how *aesthetic* production and reception relate to *nonaesthetic* communicative practices. On the basis of Adorno's analyses of the expressionist composer Arnold Schönberg, Wellmer argues that Adorno was well aware of modern art's ability to aesthetically *transmit* subjective experience. Adorno's concept of aesthetic synthesis in modern art, in which the diffuse, the nonintegrated, and the nonsensical is included in the art form itself, is in fact only possible on Adorno's own terms, Wellmer argues, in the context of a "real" utopia of violence-free communication. But this holds, Wellmer argues, only when art is attributed a mediating role in relation to forms of *nonaesthetic* communication.[81] In response to this inconsistency in Adorno, and together with Hans Robert Jauss, Wellmer wants to conceive of the artwork as the "the activating latency of a process which begins in the 'conversion of aesthetic experience into symbolic or communicative action'."[82]

Wellmer's critique of Adorno is useful to my argument because it makes clear a common strain in Habermas and Adorno: neither wants to describe art explicitly and primarily in terms of communication. Of course, they resist this account of art in quite different ways: Adorno characterizes the truth content of art in terms of the *nondiscursive* representation of the incommensurability of subjective experience; Habermas characterizes art in terms of the genuine reflection of the subjective world, and argues that art belongs to communicative reason (only) to the extent that the former's expressive validity claim is rationally *contestable.* But notwithstanding his radically different theoretical framework, and despite his own objection to Adorno's approach that is beholden to the philosophy of consciousness, Habermas himself, by limiting the object of art's validity claims to ultimately private experience, reinforces the reductive account of the communicative potential of aesthetic rationality found in Adorno.

The positive result of Wellmer's critique of Adorno and Habermas lies in his reconception of the concept of aesthetic validity and the latter's relation to other forms of validity. Wellmer initially follows Habermas's distinction of the three traditional forms of validity, when he addresses the problem of (emphatic) truth in art (*Kunstwahrheit*) offered up by Adorno's *AT.*

Wellmer is not willing to describe aesthetic validity in terms of the (propositional) truth content of an artwork, but he is similarly not prepared to reduce aesthetic rationality to expressive rationality and its respective truthfulness claims, as Habermas is. In fact, he argues, it seems intuitive that "truth" in art touches to some degree and in a peculiar way on all three forms of validity. Aesthetic validity, which Wellmer describes in term of aesthetic *coherence* (*Stimmigkeit*),

> [touches] on questions of truth, truthfuless and moral-practical correctness in an intricate manner, without it being able to be assigned to one of the three dimensions of truth or even to all three in common. The presumption seems likely that 'truth in art'—if at all—can only be saved as a *phenomenon of interference* among the dimensions of truth.[83]

Wellmer notes that Adorno had also spoken of truth in art as an interference phenomenon, namely as (1) the interlocking of the *mimetic* moment with the rational; as well as in (2) the relation between truth, aesthetic appearance (*Schein*), and reconciliation.[84] But because Adorno does not separate the two notions of truth discussed briefly above (objective truth and aesthetic coherence), his aesthetic theory remains an aesthetics of (objective) truth. For Adorno, art must be interpreted, its truth content must be (and can only be) presented, by the discursive practice of philosophy, that in turn cannot but raise truth claims about its object of inquiry, claims, however, which cannot capture the emphatic truth embodied in the artwork. Borrowing Koppe's terminology, Wellmer argues that Adorno's aesthetic theory is an "apophantic aesthetics of truth."[85] This is another way of saying, as Koppe had said, that Adorno sees truth in art as the embodiment of the emphatic form of assertory (propositional) truth.

Wellmer's reconception of truth in art as an *interference phenomenon* between the three forms of validity allows the truth content of art to be described in terms of its truth-relevant "effects" or world-disclosing potential.[86] Up to this point in my discussion of Wellmer, the terms "truth in art" and "aesthetic validity" have been used somewhat interchangeably, but the concepts they designate are clearly not identical in Wellmer's account, because (propositional) truth constitutes only *one* of the three forms of validity, the interference of which makes up aesthetic validity. His distinction between truth and "truth-relevant effects" is intended to give some contour to this distinction. In his analysis of the relation between truth in art and aesthetic validity, Wellmer holds that there is something about art that leads us to consider artworks to be bearers of truth. There is, in other words, something like a truth claim implicitly raised (and, at least implicitly, responded to) in the reception of an artwork. But this is not, strictly speaking, a claim of truth, but rather a claim of truth-potential, he argues.

Wellmer thus argues for *aesthetic validity* as a form separate from other forms of validity, one which consists in the coherence of a piece of art, which is in turn an indicator of its possible truth-effects. Wellmer understands this description of aesthetic validity as "truth in art" to represent a *metaphorical use* of the concept of truth. Moreover, Wellmer argues against the *unmetaphorical* use of the notion of truth in art:

> Truth *potential* and truth *claim* of art can [...] both only be explained with recourse to the complex interdependence of the various dimensions of truth in the experience of one's life history or the formation and change of attitudes, manners of perception and interpretation. Truth thus be can attributed to art only metaphorically.[87]

For Wellmer, the metaphorical use of the notion of truth in art is justified with the following argument: in aesthetic discourse, debate on aesthetic *coherence* (in the sense of well-formedness of the artifact) is always accompanied by a debate on the *authenticity of the presentation;* judgments with regard to the authenticity of the presentation can only be made with reference to one's own experience; but one's own experience can be mobilized in aesthetic *argumentation* only when it (one's own experience) is articulated in terms of contestable truth, rightness, and truthfulness *claims.* The concept of aesthetic validity is analogous to the concept of truth, for Wellmer, to the extent that it (aesthetic validity) is constitutive of discourse only insofar as it is at least implicitly claimed (and contestable through explicit claims). The endorsement or contestation of an artwork as *authentic,* however, extends beyond the objectively verifiable facts about its form and content to include reference to the *experience of the recipient.* To this extent, the analogy of aesthetic validity *qua authenticity* to *truth* ends where claims of aesthetic validity cannot be supported or contested with theoretical-objective arguments and must rely on rightness or truthfulness claims. Indeed, although Wellmer does not himself draw it, a further conclusion follows from his argument: that aesthetic validity has no *more* in common with truth than it does with rightness or truthfulness.

Having discharged propositional truth as the predominant form of validity in art, an assumption under which, among others, Adorno operates, Wellmer further disagrees with both Koppe and Habermas, who tend to identify aesthetic validity with truthfulness, i.e. as the kind of validity negotiated raised by expressive rationality:

> To the extent to which the metaphors of 'saying,' 'bringing-to-expression' comes to the foreground, one will try to explain the authenticity of the artwork not in terms of concepts of apophantic truth, but rather in endeëtic truthfulness; I see this tendency in Habermas and [...] in Koppe. But both of these explanations, the one through apophantic truth and the one through endeëtic truth, have the weakness in common

that they must interpret the artwork in accordance with a special type of speech act.[88]

Wellmer's rejection of the reduction of art to a speech act that raises a truthfulness claim is a general rejection of such reductions:

> Neither truth *nor* truthfulness can be assigned to the artwork *unmetaphorically* [...]. That truth and truthfulness in fact—and even normative correctness—*metaphorically* become entangled in the artwork, can only be explained by the fact that the artwork as a symbolic formation with an *aesthetic* validity claim is simultaneously the object of an *experience*, in which the three dimensions of truth are *unmetaphorically* entangled with one another.[89]

By rejecting the reducibility of aesthetic validity to any of the three fundamental forms of validity described by Habermas, Wellmer clears the way for a distinct form of aesthetic *rationality*, that operates in relative independence from the three basic forms of rationality in Habermas's account. This relative independence was not yet clearly articulated in Koppe, where aesthetic rationality is cashed out in terms of expressive rationality.

But whereas Wellmer argues for the *irreducibility* of aesthetic validity to other forms of validity, he also considers it (aesthetic validity) to be *conceptually derived* from the other three forms of validity. An unspoken presupposition in Wellmer's argument for a separate form of aesthetic validity is that the three fundamental forms of validity (the validity dimensions of truth, rightness, and truthfulness), while *analytically separable* on the basis of claims made in speech acts (which at least implicitly foreground one or the other validity dimension), are co-original (*gleichursprünglich*) in experience. I do not want to argue for or against this assumption. The last citation, however, suggests that the aesthetic form of validity reflects this original, undivided manifestation of validity (in immediate experience). In this sense, Wellmer's interference thesis characterizes aesthetic validity claims as an *obfuscation* of the validity dimensions that are discrete in speech, but one which refers to an original *unity* of these distinct validity dimensions. In all of this, it is unclear how aesthetic validity can be a *distinct* form of validity, which is conceptually *derived* from the three fundamental forms of validity, and which is nonetheless irreducible to any one *or even to any combination of those forms*.

In order to demonstrate the *uniqueness* of the aesthetic form of validity and hence its fundamental irreducibility to (any combination of) other validity forms, Wellmer turns to the *effects* of the raising of aesthetic validity claims. The uniqueness of the aesthetic form of validity lies for Wellmer lies in peculiar (potential) effects achieved through the raising of an aesthetic validity claim. Early on in his talk, Wellmer describes these as "truth-effects," and in his concluding remarks he describes their peculiarity as consisting in their fulfillment of the function of "overcoming speechlessness" with regard to experience. The *redemption* of a claim of aesthetic validity is thus reliant for Wellmer on the extra-aesthetic effects of *raising* an aesthetic validity claim. It is not clear, however, (1) whether a claim of aesthetic validity is *fully* redeemed through the mere *motivation* of discourse on formerly undiscussed complexes of experience; and (2) whether Wellmer conceives of these "truth-effects" to be perlocutionary or illocutionary in nature. Concerning (1): if aesthetic validity is supposed to represent a phenomenon of interference between the three fundamental forms of validity, then when are claims of aesthetic validity fully redeemed? This concern is called for because each of the three forms of validity is redeemed in *different* ways, on Habermas's account, an account with which, on this point at least, Wellmer agrees. That is, how can a validity claim be redeemed in which normative, theoretical-objective, and expressive validity interfere, when in isolation these validity claims are redeemed in different ways, i.e. through theoretical or ethical argumentation, through demonstration by means of consistency of actions with speech, etc. Concerning (2): is action *intersubjectively coordinated* by the raising and contestation of claims of aesthetic validity (illocution), and if so what kind of action is thus coordinated; or are the effects of raising aesthetic validity claims *external* to the aesthetic artifacts themselves (perlocutionary), since the *interference* of truth, rightness, and truthfulness would seem unlikely to yield recognizable conditions for the acceptability conditions of a validity claim?

Neither of these questions is answered in Wellmer's talk. I will not address them until 3.3, because Seel, to whose account I turn next, does address them, although he does so unsatisfactorily. Postponing my own solution to these questions until after the discussion of Seel, I will indicate, at this point, the broad outlines of my later argument. I maintain that Wellmer is right to see the *redemption* of aesthetic validity claims as in part reliant on its extra-aesthetic effects. Furthermore, I accept Wellmer's interference thesis, but insist that the nature of this interference between distinct forms of validity has to be clarified in order to provide an adequate, i.e. descriptively complete, account of the peculiarity of aesthetic rationality. I argue that aesthetic validity constitutes a phenomenon of interference between other forms of validity only in the *weak sense* that the negotiation of aesthetic validity claims (potentially) effects the *reorientation* of the recipients of aesthetic artifacts *with regard* to complexes of experience in which descriptive, normative, and expressive forms of validity interfere with one another. That is, aesthetic validity is not, as Wellmer argues, *itself* a phenomenon of interference between validity forms; rather the aesthetically valid artwork articulates experiences in which validity forms interfere.

I go on to argue that the effects that come out of the negotiation of aesthetic validity claims lies *between* illocutionary and perlocutionary effects, i.e. they belong to the third variety of effects of language that I described in the critical discussion of Habermas. In other words, the *redemption* of aesthetic validity claims consists in part in the production of effects that are implicit in institutional presuppositions, and are not *fully* internal to individual aesthetic artifacts.

There is another sense in which Wellmer's account of aesthetic validity is insufficient. He does not clearly determine whether aesthetic *validity* includes both basic senses of the word: social currency and (aesthetic) validity (*Geltung* and *Gültigkeit*). He gives an account of aesthetic validity only as actuality (*Geltung*). He argues that aesthetic validity is a separate form of validity, one which is derived from but irreducible to (any combination of) other forms of validity, but leaves open whether aesthetic validity is independent of acceptability conditions (*Gültigkeit*). As we will later see, Seel also argues that aesthetic validity is a separate, but derived, and nonetheless irreducible form thereof, but one that exists, moreover, *independent* of any acceptability conditions. Seel can work around this objection because he explicitly limits his consideration of aesthetic validity to social currency, not including (aesthetic) validity. But he also separates the redemption of aesthetic validity from the *effects* of raising an aesthetic validity claim.

Wellmer has the advantage here of requiring the full redemption of an aesthetic validity claim to rely in part on the effects of its negotiation, but he chooses the wrong effects, I argue. Wellmer's description of the function of aesthetic practice is an idealist account: the unique effect of aesthetic practice is for Wellmer limited to the articulation of previously unarticulated complexes of experience. Wellmer's concluding remarks make clear this utopian program for the societal function of art. For one, his reinterpretation of the relation between truth, aesthetic appearance, and reconciliation in Adorno's aesthetic theory is motivated, as he himself declares, by a fundamental faith in the idea of nonviolent communication. But he also identifies the specific nature of the utopic element of the aesthetic realm as the "Overcoming of speechlessness, the sensual crystallization of the abstracted meaning in experience."[90] Similar to both Koppe and Habermas, but with a different method and form of argument, Wellmer argues that aesthetic experience is indeed required by moral discourse: "without aesthetic experience and its subversive potentialities, our moral discourses would become blind and our interpretations of the world empty."[91] I agree with the interdependence between aesthetic experience and moral discourse that Wellmer argues for here, but maintain that the *unique result* of aesthetic practice and discourse does not lie in the mere articulation of previously unarticulated complexes of experience. I hold, rather, that the peculiar product of the practice of aesthetic rationality is *the recipient's reorientation with regard to her own experience* of the objective, social, and subjective worlds *in light of* the articulation of a shareable experience. Aesthetic practice, and more specifically literary practice and discourse, is not, as Wellmer argues, unique because it overcomes speechlessness: its peculiar effect is not its helping one to speak; rather it constitutes a particular *way* of speaking and reasoning, the peculiar effect of which lies in a reorientation of those who partake in aesthetic practice through the articulation of *novel ways of looking at* the objective, social, and subjective worlds.

3.2.3 Martin Seel

Martin Seel's *The Art of Disjunction*[92] understands itself as a critique of aesthetic rationality. Seel operates with a notion of human reason as comprised of various forms of rationality, of which aesthetic rationality is one constitutive form. Seel first describes the peculiar form of rationality that underlies aesthetic practice, in order to then provide an account of the role that aesthetic practice is able to play in the larger ensemble of rational practices (e.g., theoretical and normative discourses). Seel argues against the notion of human reason as dominated by any one form of rationality, by indicating the way in which all forms of rationality ultimately rely on assumptions from (and can hence be criticized from the perspective of) other forms of rationality. Seel's introductory remarks describe his understanding of human reason as an "interrational faculty of judgment": "reason is practice in switching rational perspectives."[93] *Aesthetic reason* is on Seel's account hence a misnomer if it is intended to designate anything other than aesthetic rationality as a *partial* constituent of the reasoning life.

Seel's case for reason as a nonhierarchical plurality of rationalities contradicts the Idealist (Schelling's) notion that the "highest act of reason" is "an aesthetic act"; it also speaks against Adorno's notion that the idea of truth converges with the success of aesthetic objects; and finally, it is inconsistent with the conception of aesthetic experience as somehow withdrawn from the sphere of human reason altogether (and hence not subject to rational critique). But no less than its being an only partial constituent of human reason, aesthetic rationality is also a *necessary* component thereof, on Seel's account: "Reason that is not aesthetic is not yet reason; reason that becomes aesthetic is no longer reason."[94] This attribute "aesthetic" in this sentence can be varied with the attributes "moral," "political," "expressive," "reflexive," etc. Seel's point is that the lack, exclusivity, or dominance of any one form of rationality leads to an unreasonable practice.

Habermas's *TCA* serves as a model for Seel, to the extent that it approaches the explication of the concept of reason from just such a pluralist perspective on rationality. At the same time, Seel finds Habermas's "communicative threeness and trinity of reason" a product of over-systematization and unconvincing as an account of actual communicative functions.[95] Whereas Seel criticizes the way in which Habermas's defends reason against its critics, however, he also stresses his intent to criticize the aestheticist critique of reason (*á la* late Romanticism, Nietzsche, certain varieties of postmodernism, etc.): "The critique of aesthetic rationality to which I wish to contribute here, not only *must*, it *can* consummate itself as a critique of reason *dominated* by aesthetics."[96]

Seel's discussion of aesthetic rationality begins with an account of Kant's *CJ* as, to bring it to a point, the source of all subsequent confusion concerning the rationality of aesthetic practice. Seel points out that Kant distinguishes two kinds of aesthetic judgment, primary valuations (judgment of taste), and secondary valuations, which consist in *elaborations* of primary valuations, through *explication,* into "speculative knowledge." Seel argues that with this analysis Kant produces an absurd division of labor between the spontaneous and the reflexive aspects of aesthetic judgment, between pure and intellectualized interest in the beautiful.[97] Kant's *Critique of Judgment* focuses almost exclusively on the first of these aspects and devotes minimal attention to the logic of the second, reflexive aspect of aesthetic judgment. Because of his one-sided account, Seel argues, Kant does not see aesthetic artifacts as possible objects in a rationally conducted debate that would ultimately turn on more than the mere preferences of the participants in the debate.

Seel holds that the fundamental problems evident in all subsequent accounts of the relation between aesthetic judgment and rationality are prefigured in Kant's construction and resolution of the antinomy of taste in §§56–57 of *CJ.* This antinomy goes as follows:

> The judgment of taste is not grounded in concepts; for otherwise one could dispute it (determine through proof) [...]. The judgment of taste is grounded in concepts, for otherwise one could not, regardless of the variety of the same, even argue over it (lay claim to the necessary agreement of others with this judgment).

Kant resolves this antinomy by pointing out the ambiguity of the expressions *concept* and *criterion* (*Begriff* and *Kriterium*). Kant insists that aesthetic judgment relies on indefinite concepts (*unbestimmte Begriffe*). Definite concepts (*bestimmte Begriffe*), on the other hand, can never be the basis of aesthetic judgments. The "indefinite concept of reason," and *not* "definite concepts of reason," is the basis for intersubjective agreement concerning aesthetic judgments. This "indeterminate" concept of reason signifies for Kant the "supersensual substrate of humanity." With this Kant means the predisposition of humans to autonomously determine their actions (and by extension, their predilection for private preferences). The function of the exchange of aesthetic judgments for Kant consists in the communicative self-reassurance among humans of a common sensoria for the possibilities of an "appropriate happiness."[98] Aesthetic judgments do not after all aim at knowledge, for Kant, but rather at the actuality and actualizability of a "feeling of life" (*Lebensgefühl*).[99] Seel maintains that although the question posed by Kant is the right one, his anthropological solution to the antinomy of taste, and that the attendant separation of argumentation and aesthetic judgment, is the source of all the problematic accounts of the relation between rationality and aesthetic practice that have followed: "That the central question of §56 of *CJ* is correctly *asked,* but still insufficiently answered, from this comes the concern of the question about the rationality of the aesthetic."[100] The precise question that remains unsatisfactorily answered by Kant's solution to the antinomy of taste is the following: how do I know that a given *object* is the condition of my free contemplation (*Bedingung meines freien Betrachtens*) and that it is not merely on the basis of my private *preference* that this object pleases me?

Seel identifies two general approaches to aesthetic theory that he understands as more or less direct consequences of Kant's antinomy, approaches that he designates aesthetics of withdrawal (*Entzugsästhetik*) and aesthetics of overbidding (*Überbietungsästhetik*). The first of these argues against a specifically aesthetic form of rationality in favor of a notion of aesthetic perception completely free of the restraints of a cognitive understanding of the world; for the aesthetics of withdrawal there is (or should be) no *logic* of aesthetic argumentation because such a grounding of aesthetic objects would (unfairly) reduce aesthetic objects to meanings foreign to them or unable to fully capture them. Nietzsche, P. Valéry, G. Bataille, W. Iser, R. Bubner, and, not surprisingly, Kant (of the "Analytik" of aesthetic judgment), are proponents of this kind of aesthetic theory. The second of these, the aesthetics of overbidding, also argues against a specifically aesthetic form of rationality, but does so in favor of an integrated notion of truth and cognition. Supporters of the aesthetics of overbidding argue that there is no independent logic of aesthetic argumentation because aesthetic experience is an outstanding (if not the superior) form of (emphatic) cognition. Schelling, the young Hegel, Heidegger, Adorno, and Gadamer are representatives of this kind of aesthetic theory. Seel's account rejects both the aesthetics of withdrawal and the aesthetics of overbidding, to the extent that it sees aesthetic experience neither (1) as impermeable to rationality nor (2) as the pinnacle of cognition. This is the false alternative that Seel sees as arising from Kant's antinomy.

Seel similarly criticizes two recent attempts to break up this false alternative: (a) Karl-Heinz Bohrer's aesthetics of "suddenness"[101] and (b) Koppe's endeëtic aesthetics, discussed above:

(a) Bohrer's Nietzsche-inspired aesthetic theory *synthesizes* the aesthetics of withdrawal and the aesthetics of overbidding by, on the one hand, insisting on the autonomy and irreducibility of aesthetic experience (*Schein*), while, on the other hand, asserting the cognitive effect of "sudden" (i.e. aesthetic) perception. Bohrer's essays on the aesthetics of suddenness deploy terms such as *fantasy truth* (Phantasiewahrheit)[102] reflexion of the present (Gegenwarts-Reflexion),[103] and "the deeper knowledge of the world [through aesthetic experience],"[104] in order to indicate the mutual imbrication of (emphatic) cognitive truth and (autonomous) aesthetic experience in the moment that he is arguing for. I cannot treat Bohrer's aesthetic theory any more fully here, other than to point out the way in which he justifies his account of aesthetic experience as (1) radically *withdrawn* from a discourse that aims at establishing objective truth; and one which simultaneously (2) *overbids* the everyday notion of objective truth: in a typically deconstructionist manner, Bohrer insists that the inconsistency of his position is precisely the point: "The paradox shall be."[105]

(b) Koppe's endeëtic aesthetic theory, by way of contrast, has the merit for Seel of avoiding the opposition between a withdrawn purity of aesthetic experience on the one hand and a superior truth in aesthetic experience on the other hand, by demonstrating that aesthetic truth, i.e. the peculiar quality born by the paradigmatic articulation of human needs, stands in a dialectical relationship to discursive (be it practical or theoretical) communication. For Koppe, the peculiarity of aesthetically successful artifacts consists in their actualization of expressive rationality: aesthetic artifacts are successful for Koppe when they articulate situations as situations of human need through presentations of experiences that are fundamentally *shareable*. But whereas Habermas's account of aesthetic rationality has the problem of describing the latter in terms of the *intersubjective* attribution (or abrogation) of authenticity to articulations of ultimately private *subjective* complexes of experience (see 3.1); Koppe's account of aesthetic rationality has a different weakness: it limits the aesthetic function to an expressivity that bears a communicative character to the extent that it articulates a *particular* shareable human need: I have described this limitation above (see 3.2.1). Seel rightly sees Koppe's account of the dialectical relation between aesthetic and nonaesthetic forms of rationality as an improvement on Habermas's account of aesthetic rationality as mere expressive rationality. Seel also correctly identifies a further fault in Koppe's account: seeing the *peculiarity* of aesthetic practice as consisting in its communicative *continuity* with other modes of rationally motivated, linguistically mediated practice. Koppe's account of aesthetic practice as an articulation of shareable situations of need paradoxically thus renders aesthetic practice both autonomous and a handmaiden of communicative reason. Seel wants to eliminate this inconsistency in Koppe by doing away with both the autonomy notion and the handmaiden role.

Bohrer's and Koppe's aesthetic theories, each argue, in quite different ways, against the mutually exclusive *alternative* of the aesthetics of overbidding and the aesthetics of withdrawal. Bohrer does so with an account of the aesthetic moment as fully *discontinuous* with communicative reason; Koppe does so with an account of aesthetic perception as fundamentally bound up with shareable situations of need, and hence as *continuous* with communicative reason. Against these solutions, Seel argues that aesthetic perception is neither *fundamentally* continuous nor *fundamentally* discontinuous with communicative reason. It can be either, depending on circumstances. This insight is useful for my argument to the extent that Seel supports it with a subsequent account of the peculiar rationality on the basis of which the communicative character of any particular aesthetic practice can be determined.

Seel sees the aesthetic relevance of Bohrer's and Koppe's respective notions of suddenness and concernment converge in the concept of aesthetic *experience,* which is the fundamental concept on which his account of aesthetic rationality will turn. Seel wants to give an account of aesthetic bearing (*ästhetisches Verhalten*) as a bearing toward articulated phenomena that make present (*vergegenwärtigen*) the experiential content (*Erfahrungsgehalt*) of situations and simultaneously distance themselves from those situations.[106] In other words, the aesthetic moment, for Seel, is one in which the experiential content of situations is articulated, whereby these situations do not fully converge with the situation in which they are articulated. Here is where Seel's mediation of Koppe and Bohrer becomes evident: aesthetic perception is the apprehension of the *momentary nature* (suddenness) and the *context of existential meaningfulness* (concernment) of situations distinct from the situation in which aesthetic perception occurs. Aesthetic phenomena have, for Seel, the unique character of experiences in which one experiments with another (and hence with one's own) experience.[107]

Seel is well aware of the obscurity of the concept of aesthetic experience in his Heideggerian formulation and endeavors to clarify it. The uniqueness of *aesthetic* experience as a form of experience turns on the relation between experience and situation, Seel argues. At the same time, the relation between experience and situation may not be described only in terms of any *particular* kind of perception or action. In first directing attention to the general question of the relation between experience and situation, in order to account for the role of this relation in aesthetic practice, Seel follows a directive given by John Dewey in the latter's *Art as Experience,*[108] where he suggests that the question of the peculiar meaning of artworks is best approached by provisionally forgetting art in order to examine the general conditions of experience.

Here I cannot trace in sufficient detail Seel's meticulous, phenomenologically and hermeneutically informed account of the relation between experience and situation, and can only offer a simplifying synopsis.[109] Seel begins by distinguishing his definition of (lifeworld) experience from empiricist accounts of experience as nothing other than the perceptual registration of objects and events. Lifeworld experience, by contrast, is distinct from such a form of experience by virtue of its situation-disclosing character (*situationserschließender Charakter*): having an experience is not a matter of merely recognizing changes in states of affairs or heretofore unrecognized states of affairs, but rather of entering into a practically different relation to the world. Experiences are occasioned by events that cause prior expectations of behavior to collapse, and are consummated through the finding of an orientation appropriate to the concerned situation. The product of such attempts at reorientation are new views on the world (*Einstellungen*). "Views on the world" are understood by Seel to be generalized appraisals of situations (*generalisierte Situationseinschätzungen*) through which we practically relate to the world. These views on the world are comprised of our volitive, cognitive, and emotional ways of relating to the world (*Weltbezüge*) and their combination comprises an orienting knowledge (*Orientierungwisssen*). The counterpart to this generalized, orienting knowledge is the experiential content (*Erfahrungsgehalt*) in a new situation. The uniqueness of a situation becomes meaningful in the latter's experiential content (for a subject), which in turn takes form against background orienting knowledge (of that subject).

With the concept of experiential content that he draws out of the analysis of the relation between experience and situation, Seel is able to make the move to defining the specificity of *aesthetic* experience. He does this by addressing the question of how experiential content can be communicated. He first describes two forms of articulation that are *unable* to sufficiently relay experiential content: (1) the thematizing (*thematisierend*) and (2) the visualizing (*vergegenwärtigend*) modes of articulation. Through the *thematizing* mode of articulation we represent experiences by means of propositionally differentiated systems of signification (e.g., natural languages). Through the *visualizing* mode of articulation we represent a situation with the help of indicative actions (*Zeigehandlungen*). Because both of these modes of articulation necessarily abstract from the situation they represent and hence cannot capture the meaningfulness of it, Seel wants to posit a third mode of articulation to account for the peculiarity of aesthetic experience, the presentative (*präsentativ*). This is the mode of articulation of artworks, for instance, and it makes present to the recipient, Seel argues, all those ways of relating to the world that are present in an experience. Instead of just presenting partial aspects of a situation, the (successful) artwork articulates all that distinguishes the meaningfulness of a particular situation.

Hence, for Seel, aesthetic experience distinguishes itself from nonaesthetic experience to the extent that its object is *another experience*. The experience had[110] through the comprehension of aesthetic objects is determined by a *doubled situation:* a situation in which another situation is made present to perception. Whereas the view gained through having a nonaesthetic experience has direct bearing on individual, concrete, practical situations, the change in orientation (*Einstellungskorrektur*) and world-disclosure (*Welterschließung*) resulting from aesthetic experiences are of a purely projective nature, i.e. constitute a perceptual *distantiation* from practice. Furthermore, as indicated above, the aesthetic experience itself is not, for Seel, coextensive with the experience presented through the aesthetic object. The aesthetic object allows the recipient to experience not simply her/his own act of perception, but rather the context of meaningfulness of *another situation*. Seel writes: "The successful object does not mean the aesthetic experience, it means the experience that aesthetically comes to be experienced. Those who experience aesthetically do not experience their own, present experience, they experience a situation in their world."[111] In other words, aesthetic experience is *not* merely the reflexive experience of one's own experience of an object; rather, the aesthetic object is an object of perception that successfully enables the experience of another experience; experiencing another experience, which consists in recognizing the context of meaningfulness of another situation, results, in accordance with the definition of "having an experience" as outlined above, in a *change in orientation* of the recipient of the aesthetic object, which, in turn, through her/his situated exposure to a novel situation, consists in a revision of her/his *generalized appraisals* of situations.

With his thesis of the *situatedness* of aesthetic experience in the lifeworld of the recipient, Seel hopes to counter both the aesthetics of withdrawal and the aesthetics of overbidding: aesthetic experience is neither separate from other ways of experiencing the world (aesthetics of withdrawal), nor a complete or unifying mode of experiencing (aesthetics of overbidding).[112] Rather, aesthetic experience, for Seel, is a *distinct* form of experience with regard both to (1) its object (another experience); and to (2) its result (a *contemplative* change in view, i.e. one without immediate practical consequences).

I argue that Seel's notion of the nonpractical reorientation of the recipient of aesthetic objects does not provide for an adequate account of the effects of aesthetic practice, and fails in this regard in several senses:

1. it does not describe the specificity of the effects of aesthetic practice, because there are other nonaesthetic experiences that result in "reorientation" *and* that do not have immediate practical consequences (e.g., the adoption of a novel maxim of action in the wake of an unusually difficult practical situation, such as a moral dilemma, and which would not be likely to apply again in the near future);
2. it artificially limits the redemption of aesthetic validity claims to the *actual* reorientation of the recipients of aesthetic objects, and thus limits aesthetic validity to social currency (*Geltung*), to the exclusion of validity (*Gültigkeit*) (e.g., in addition to the resonance demonstrably produced in a reading audience by an aesthetically well-formed piece of literature, one can equally well imagine an artwork with a legitimate aesthetic validity claim that has not achieved its deserved public resonance);
3. because it limits the redemption of aesthetic validity claims to *nonpractical* reorientation, Seel's account, in an odd coherence with Habermas's account, strictly excludes "perlocutionary" effects of any sort from the (aesthetically) legitimate effects of aesthetic practice.

I further argue:

4. that Seel cannot consistently hold both:
    (a) that aesthetic practice reorients the recipients of aesthetic artifacts in their view of the world, a reorientation that is irreducible to

theoretical-instrumental,   moral-practical,   and   subjective-preferential ways of relating to the world, or any combination thereof;
(b) that aesthetic experience is *not* a unifying form of experience.

I argue that one both can and should understand the meta-level reorientation that results from aesthetic experience as a *unifying* form of experience,
without giving in to the aesthetics of overbidding and claiming a *superior*
form of knowledge (or emphatic form of truth) to be gained through aesthetic practice. I return to objections 3 and 4 to Seel's account later in this
section.

In the meantime, I will prepare my argument by showing how Seel
responds to possible objections to his account. Of particular relevance to my
argument are the objections that he formulates from the perspective of a
communicative theory of aesthetic practice. Habermas and Koppe, as
representatives of this theoretical approach to aesthetic practice, see the
peculiarity of aesthetic practice as lying in the fact that in aesthetic artifacts
situations are offered up in a succinct form that adequately reflects the
experience of those involved in those situations. For Habermas and Koppe
the aesthetically successful artwork is not only *truthful* (as is any fitting
expressive utterance, i.e. *Erlebnissatz*); it is also an *authentic* expression,
which means that it articulates a shareable view of the world *in light of*
subjective experience (i.e. it is *paradigmatic* for the self-understanding of a
group, society, or epoch). For the communicative theory of aesthetic practice, the aesthetically successful is the authentic, and the authentic is a
function of expressivity.[113] Seel, by way of contrast, insists that aesthetic
articulation (i.e. the presentation of experiential content) can by no means
by reduced to one of the elementary forms of communicative articulation
(descriptive, normative, or expressive). Indeed, aesthetic articulation constitutes its own form of articulation. Seel does not clarify, however, at least
in *AD*, whether aesthetic articulation constitutes a fully distinct, fourth
fundamental form of articulation, or whether it is a distinct form to the
extent that it *combines* the three fundamental forms. I later return to this
issue.

Seel argues that the irreducibility of aesthetic articulation to any elementary form of communicative articulation calls into question the communicative nature of aesthetic signs in general. In agreement with Adorno, Seel
refuses to describe the *artwork* in terms of communication. Aesthetic *practice*, on the other hand, should be analyzed (inter alia) in terms of communication. The communicative aspect of art is not, Seel argues, to be found in
works of art, but rather in the forms of art criticism. Aesthetic interest, or,
more exactly, human interest in aesthetic artifacts, does not manifest itself
solely in the private *reception* of artifacts, but also in the *explication* of the
experiences presented in and had through those artifacts. Habermas sees the
explicative role of art criticism similarly, but maintains that not only the
artists, but also the art critic, in her bearing in relation to the aesthetic

artifact, orients herself primarily toward the validity claim of truthfulness.[114] Seel contends (1) that the explication of the aesthetic object in terms of aesthetic success (or failure) in fact relies on *all* of the dimensions of validity, and moreover (2) that such explication relies on none of these dimensions becoming predominant.[115] Seel supports the first part of this claim by rightly arguing that a careful look at actual aesthetic criticism, of works of literature, for instance, shows that aesthetic argumentation just as well avails itself of statements that make theoretical and moral or ethical-preferential validity claims as it does of statements that refer either (1) to the truthfulness of the work at hand (i.e. evaluations of a presumed truthfulness claim on the part of the author), or (2) to one's own immediate experience of the work or to the work's speaking to one's own biography (the recipients' own truthfulness claims). Seel correctly argues that the kinds of validity claims raised and contested in aesthetic critique vary greatly, and are not reducible to (and cannot even be characterized primarily in terms of) a form of the truthfulness claim, as Habermas argues.

But the second part of Seel's aforementioned claim concerning the lack of the dominance of claims of any particular form of validity in aesthetic criticism is deeply problematic. Seel writes:

> The exact analysis of the foundations of aesthetic critique makes clear that its explicative capacity to substantiate stands or falls—or rather increases or decreases—, to the extent that none of the nonaesthetic dimensions of validity gains the upper hand in it. Precisely here is the root of the meaning of aesthetic validity. Precisely here the possibility is grounded to judge and negotiate the appropriateness of perceptions beyond the ban of its immediately reality-forming effectiveness.[116]

When one recalls Seel's introductory remarks on the appropriate understanding of human reason as both (1) a being accustomed to *alternating* between rational perspectives; and (2) a providing for the possibility of interrational critique (i.e. theoretical critique of practical arguments, the normative critique of aesthetic arguments, etc), it seems that Seel has, in the end, aligned aesthetic critique with the overarching concept of reason in which no particular form of rationality is supposed to become dominant. This was precisely the kind of equivocation that he had claimed to set out against in arguing against the possibility of aesthetic *reason* (and *for* an aesthetic *rationality* that is a constitutive component of human reason): "Reason that is not aesthetic is not yet reason; reason that becomes aesthetic is no longer reason."[117] If the *peculiar* sense of aesthetic validity consists in none of the nonaesthetic dimensions of validity becoming dominant; and furthermore if an appropriate understanding of human reason holds that no form of rationality should dominate human practices; then there is little in Seel's argument to disallow the conclusion that aesthetic rationality is the meta-rationality that regulates the proper balance of other rationalities. This clearly leads to the aesthetics of overbidding that Seel alleges to discharge.

The last part of the citation at the top of the previous paragraph is perhaps even more odd: aesthetic rationality's capacity to pass judgment on and negotiate the appropriateness of ways of looking at the world without consideration of the potential real effects of adopting those ways of looking at the world clearly exempts aesthetic rationality from the strictures it would be subject to in the domain of the theoretical-instrumental and moral-practical forms of rationality, respectively. And this clearly leads to the aesthetics of withdrawal that Seel equally alleges to set out against. "For perceptions and views on the world are substantiated only aesthetically:"[118] this citation encapsulates Seel's understanding of the peculiarity of aesthetic judgment. It also demonstrates the fundamental contradiction in Seel's account of aesthetic rationality as, on the one hand, *one* distinct form of rationality in a nonhierarchical arrangement of mutually complementary forms of rationality, and, on the other hand, *the* form of rationality the operation of which legitimates or invalidates a particular perspective on a situation.

Despite the problems of inconsistency in Seel's account here, it is motivated by a valid concern with regard to Habermas's conception of the complementary relation between cognitive-instrumental rationality, moral-practical rationality, and aesthetic-expressive rationality. Seel argues, as mentioned above, that the complementarity of the relationship between different forms of rationality consists in the possibility of *interrational critique.* Habermas is not able to theorize the relation in this way, because he considers the three types of rationality as corresponding to three fundamental forms of validity, which are in turn independent from one another, although *coexistent* in every speech act. Seel argues for distinguishing the fundamental forms of rationality as forms of grounding *practices,* and not as forms of grounding the acceptability of individual speech acts. This allows one, he argues, as Habermas's approach does not, to sufficiently account for the need and possibility of different forms of rationality to be complemented by one another. Descriptive and evaluative *statements,* in different contexts and serving different functions, count as relevant *grounds* (and may in turn rely on or be accompanied by expressive statements). But it is the arguments made for *priorities* of grounding *maxims of behavior* that lay claim to different forms of *validity,* not the descriptive and evaluative statements themselves, Seel argues. The different forms of validity are connected to each other to the extent that the assumptions concerning the priority of any form of validity bring all the forms of validity into a weighted relationship in the context of a particular practice. Although he does not himself offer a comprehensive argument for the assertion, Seel claims that assumptions from the realm of the other forms of rationality quite often play a decisive role in the mode of argumentation of any particular form of rationality.[119] Hence the complementarity of the forms of rationality as well as their mutual criticizability, on Seel's account.

Seel's argument that the forms of rationality are ways of grounding *practices,* and not primarily ways of grounding the acceptability of individual *speech acts* is useful to my argument because it lets one describe a practice that is irreducible to standard forms of speech acts, such as the production, reception, and critique of literary texts, as a rational practice. Seel's account offers further support to my argument above (see 3.1.1) that establishing the unique contribution of a rational practice (here literary culture) to communicative reason by no means requires that that practice be describable in terms of discrete speech acts.[120] His argument that any form of rationality makes assumptions about the *priority* of the relevance of some form of validity to a given practice, and *not* that any particular form of rationality negotiates exclusively *one kind* of validity claim, lets us describe literary rationality as being involved, to some extent, like all other forms of rationality, with the negotiation of claims of *all* the fundamental forms of validity. I will return to the discussion of the peculiarity of the aesthetic validity claim shortly, and present my own account of it in the next section (3.3). My argument with regard to the nature of aesthetic validity claim is inspired in part by Wellmer's thesis of aesthetic validity as a phenomenon of interference, but as argued above (see 3.2.2), aesthetic validity is not, as Wellmer argues, *itself* a phenomenon of interference between validity forms; rather the aesthetically valid artwork articulates experiences in which validity forms interfere.

Just as Seel offers an insightful critique of Habermas's account of aesthetic rationality as centered on the negotiation of a form of the truthfulness claim, his account also offers valid objections to Wellmer's revision of Habermas. Seel considers it vital to a nonhierarchically pluralist notion of reason that one dismiss the claims of a utopic account of aesthetic practice. First, Seel rejects Wellmer's description of the utopic function art as the "Überwindung der Sprachlosigkeit." Seel is not prepared to set up art solely as the handmaiden of communicative reason, even though he concedes that it may often take on such a function, (i.e. present *relevant* experiential content *that cannot be otherwise relayed*—through thematization or visualization in Seel's use of those terms—in the context of the discussion of particular issues of generalizable concern).

Seel also rejects the second utopic element of Wellmer's account of the function of art, as producing the "the sensual crystallization of the abstracted meaning in experience,"[121] as such a notion sets up aesthetic experience as an emphatic (i.e. superior) form of experience, as it is in Adorno. Seel prefers to see the regulative component of the experience of art as a *nonutopic regulative.* In line with his description of aesthetic experience as experimentation, through the experience of another experience, with one's own experience, Seel describes this nonutopic regulative thus: "Experience! (for experience's sake)."[122] Aesthetic experience is not *per se* bound to any other, external purpose, only to the reflexive experience of experience. This at once determines its uniqueness and its *digressive potential* when it is not brought into a relation to coordinate other forms of action. The communicative utopia that Habermas and (particularly) Wellmer envision for aesthetic practice is, Seel claims, essentially a political one, not an aesthetic one, hence one that "instrumentalizes" aesthetic practice for normative projects.[123] Seel's argument here underscores his earlier point that aesthetic practice is neither *fundamentally* continuous with communicative reason nor *fundamentally* discontinuous with communicative reason. Seel is right to the extent that he points out that there are noncommunicative aesthetic artifacts (and, by extension, noncommunicative *uses* of aesthetic artifacts). But *literary* artifacts, I argue, by virtue of their linguistic medium, are always produced and presented to a public as communicative acts. This does not mean that literature is per se a form of communicative action, but that literary culture is a *forum* for communicative reason: that literary artifacts be taken as communicative acts is an unassailable presupposition in the acts of producing, presenting, reading, and criticizing literary texts, I argue.

A more recent article by Seel extends and modifies some of his arguments from *AD,* and is relevant to my study to the extent that it addresses the question of whether there exists a separate form of aesthetic validity and the nature of the relation of such a form of validity to other forms of validity. In "Art, Truth and World-Disclosure,"[124] Seel argues both against (1) the premises of truth aesthetics (the aesthetics of outbidding of Adorno & Co.) which he had begun in *TCA* and an account of which I have given above; and against (2) the notion of truth in art as a derived form of truth. Proponents of the latter notion fall into two subcamps: the first of these denies the existence of a form of aesthetic validity distinct from the fundamental forms of truth, rightness, and truthfulness, and is represented by Habermas in *TCA;*[125] the second posits the existence of a separate form of aesthetic validity (despite truth in art being a derived form of truth, i.e. despite "truth in art" amounting to an only metaphorical use of the term *truth*), and is represented by Wellmer and post-*TCA* Habermas. The *common* position here is that truth in art is derived, i.e. that the term *truth* applies to art only in a metaphorical sense; the *difference* between these two versions lies in the question whether there is a separate form of aesthetic validity. Wellmer says "yes," Habermas says or implies both "yes" and "no." Seel argues against both of these accounts, arguing both that there *is* a separate form of aesthetic validity, and that *neither* the validity of artworks *nor* the truth of art-critical statements constitutes a *derived* form of truth.

Seel sets off by pointing out that validity can exist outside of validity claims. He demonstrates this by distinguishing between assertory truth and validity. Whereas true assertions can be made about nonpropositional knowledge or about something that is nonpropositionally valid, the truth of such an assertion is not necessarily the same as the *validity* of the object about which true assertions can be made. An artwork, for instance, is not valid only to the extent that true statements can be made about it. More exactly, the aesthetic validity of an artwork is a different quality than the truth of assertions that can be made about it. Seel holds to his argument from *TCA* that aesthetic judgments can in fact be grounded, and *not only* by means of making true statements about the artwork. Aesthetic judgments can be grounded through an interpretive process that consists in explicating the success (*Gelungenheit*) or failure of an aesthetic object.

"Truth in art" is understood by Seel to be a *mode* of aesthetic validity; and aesthetic validity in turn is understood as determined by the assertability, discussability, and demonstrability of intersubjective values (as opposed to the quality referred to in the pronouncement that one likes or prefers something). Seel hence argues for an account of aesthetic validity as a kind of social validity (*soziale Geltung*): aesthetic validity exists to the extent that intersubjective values are being negotiated, irrespective of whether a validity claim is raised. Seel continues by clarifying what he means by "intersubjective values": they are, obviously, *not* merely subjective preferences, as already mentioned, but they also cannot be adequately described by truth or rightness claims. In *questions of taste*, for instance, the intersubjective values under discussion concern certain styles of life, and on the basis of these value orientations the specifically *aesthetic* function fulfilled through discussions of taste (and the actions coordinated by these discussions) is a stylization or beautification of human life.[126] This kind of discussion reveals a peculiar form of aesthetic validity, not evident, Seel claims, in purely *contemplative* aesthetic practice, the significance of which lies precisely in its nonevaluative stance toward certain objects. That is to say, the contemplation of objects does not alone reveal any peculiar form of aesthetic validity, because any brick or bell can serve as an object of contemplation. But the addition of *stylization* to *contemplation* still does not provide for an adequate account of the aesthetic function of *art* specifically: although the perception and evaluation of art is invariably bound up with questions of taste, the function of art is also just not the stylization or beautification of life, because this function can also be served by my silver coffee service or my new BMW.

Seel argues that the special function of art, and that aspect that renders it a unique field of aesthetic practice, is the perception and articulation of ways-the-world-is (*Weltweisenwahrnehmung* and *Weltweisenartikulation*). Seel identifies the four aspects of the perception of ways-the-world-is as the visualization (*Vergegenwärtigung*) of:

1. the existential meaningfulness of conditions and events for human experience and expectations;
2. the construction of patterns and signs in which operations of human perception, comprehension, and articulation can be rendered;
3. the materials and media, processes, and human capacities through which (1) and (2) are realized; and

4. the meaningfulness of the experience of *art* for human experience and
    expectations (this self-reflexive activity of art is a subset of [1]).

Seel argues that whereas any one of these functions can be fulfilled through
other practices, the techniques of their realization are not thinkable without
the history and experience of art. This is so, he argues, because art is
"institutionalized perceptions of ways-the-world-is."[127] He further spec-
ulates that art fulfills each of the three main functions by virtue of fulfilling
the other functions, and in this, he argues, lies its (art's) peculiarity and its
constitutive and central function. Seel will later endeavor to ground the
various strong assumptions made in the above exposition, an explication
I do not recapitulate here. This particular exposition is important for my
study to the extent that Seel describes art as a unique practice that synthesizes (articulates through aesthetic artifacts) all of the constitutive aspects of
perceiving ways-the-world-is. That he ultimately relies on an historical
argument for the special societal function of art in doing so is irrelevant to
my argument. What is important for my argument is Seel's thesis that the
revelation and/or production of novel views on the world, which is the
unique function of art properly understood, is moreover the basis for evaluating the aesthetic *validity* of an artwork. Further key to Seel's conception
of the aesthetic validity of an artwork is that the capacity to reveal or produce novel views on the world is *fully independent* of that artwork's
descriptive, prescriptive, and expressive content. Hence the independence of
aesthetic validity from other forms of validity, for Seel.

For this reason Seel challenges Wellmer's thesis that "truth in art" constitutes a phenomenon of interference between the nonaesthetic dimensions
of validity (truth, rightness, and truthfulness). Insofar as "truth in art" is a
product of such an interference for Wellmer, he considers truth in art to be a
relational form of truth. And to the extent that Wellmer describes the nature
of truth in art as a relational truth, he gives an account of truth in art as
derived. That Wellmer sees "truth in art" as a derived form of truth is furthermore evident in his underscoring the *metaphorical* nature of the application of the term *truth* to art. Wellmer argues that this metaphorical
application of *truth* to art is justified not so much to the extent that art is a
bearer of truth, but rather insofar as art has truth-*potential* through its
world-disclosing capacity. This truth-potential is the basis for evaluating the
aesthetic validity of an artwork. That is, the aesthetic validity of an artwork
is to be measured in terms of its capacity to produce truth-effects. Wellmer
also describes this capacity as identical to an artwork's resonance
(*Stimmigkeit*). For Wellmer, "truth in art" is the validity of world-disclosure
(*Geltung der Welterschließung*): "truth in art" lies in art's capacity to render
heretofore unrecognized aspects of the world *in such a way that subsequent
action on the part of the recipient(s) is coordinated in light of this rendering.*
Hence the "truth-potential" of art. And hence the dependence of aesthetic
validity on other forms of validity: an artwork is aesthetically valid for

Wellmer only if it creates, through the effect of its world-disclosing force on the perception of the recipient, potential for actual change, through that recipient, in the world.

Seel wants to challenge this definition of aesthetic validity on the basis of the role it ascribes to world-disclosure. He asserts that Wellmer's definition of aesthetic validity as the validity of world-disclosure assigns both too much and too little validity to art. Wellmer assigns too *little* validity to art because he leaves unexplained how the *aesthetic* disclosure of the world is distinct from *nonaesthetic* disclosure of the world, Seel argues. On this point he cites Charles Taylor, who argues in "Language and Society"[128] that the linguistic potential of world-disclosure is by no means a capacity that is peculiar to aesthetic practice. On the other hand, Seel argues, Wellmer assigns too *much* validity to art because aesthetic validity (understood as the validity of world-disclosure) becomes the circular construct of "the validity of validity" when one understands world-disclosure, as Wellmer does, as the process of acquiring a novel understanding of reality through the interference of *the various nonaesthetic dimensions of validity*. Common to both of Seel's objections, too much and, alternately, too little validity for art, is the discomfort with there being no distinct *and* independent form of aesthetic validity. *This* aim, I argue, the aim to establish the independence of aesthetic validity, and *not* the aim to avoid circularity in the definition of aesthetic validity, is the more fundamental motivation behind Seel's opposition to the definition of aesthetic validity as the validity of world-disclosure. It is only in the face of the task of establishing the *independence* of aesthetic validity that the definition of aesthetic validity as the validity of world-disclosure as described above becomes circular. Whereas Wellmer is content to posit a *distinct* form of aesthetic validity that is nonetheless *dependent* on nonaesthetic validity forms to the extent that it consists in a *relation* between these; Seel wants to posit a distinct form of aesthetic validity that is also *fully independent* from and hence cannot be described in terms of extra-aesthetic forms of validity or any relation between them at all.

Seel essentially criticizes Wellmer's definition of aesthetic validity as the validity of world-disclosure as not going far enough in revising Habermas's argument that aesthetic validity is a form of expressive truthfulness, and hence not even a *distinct* form of validity. Seel keenly illustrates the problem with defining aesthetic validity as a *derivation* from nonaesthetic forms of validity, as Wellmer does, with the example of Habermas's reception of Wellmer. In response to Wellmer's critique of his limitation of aesthetic validity to truthfulness, Habermas responds in two ways simultaneously. On the one hand, he accepts Wellmer's notion of truth in *art* specifically as a phenomenon of interference between nonaesthetic dimensions of validity, although he leaves all other instances of aesthetic validity (*non*artistic instances thereof), in the realm of expressive rationality;[129] on the other hand, Habermas raises art to a unique status as the "pure form" of world-disclosure.[130] Seel points out how this view of the role of art as the avant-garde of world-disclosure flatly contradicts Habermas's earlier claim that art relies essentially on an "validity oriented toward the internal world."[131] In *TCA* the validity claims of art are centered on truthfulness claims and there is no *distinct* form of aesthetic validity. In *TCA*, truthfulness claims refer solely to the realm of subjective experience, and have neither constative nor normative content, i.e. they refer directly to neither the objective nor the social worlds. But Habermas cannot simultaneously hold that art centers on truthfulness claims and that it is an unadulterated motor of world-disclosure, without contradicting himself (if the "world" contained in "world-disclosure" encompasses the objective, social, *and* subjective worlds, which is indeed how Habermas understands the term). Indeed, Habermas's double position on truth in art leads right back to Kant's problematic solution of the antinomy of taste, Seel argues: Habermas reverses his earlier position by claiming that the aesthetic validity of art *is* its own form of validity, but he does not give an account of how aesthetic validity relates to the three fundamental forms of validity. In Habermas's incomplete self-revision, "truth in art" ends up being its own form of validity in virtue of its not being its own form of validity, a clearly absurd position.

In some sense Wellmer's account of aesthetic validity takes a similarly dubious position. Seel wants to clear up Wellmer's problematic definition of aesthetic validity as the validity of world-disclosure by breaking up the direct link between validity-orientation and world-disclosure that Wellmer inherits from Habermas. Seel wants to argue not just that the process of world-disclosure does not necessarily presuppose the negotiation of validity *claims,* as indicated earlier, but rather also that not all forms of validity-oriented practice necessarily have world-disclosure as their immediate aim. Seel proposes his solution to the problem of aesthetic validity's independence by describing the unique function of art as the disclosure of world-disclosure (*Erschließung der Welterschließung*): "Does not the specific aesthetic mission of art lie in creating situations in which situations from our experience can be experienced?"[132] Seel's question is rhetorical: he means that the peculiar function of art lies not only nor primarily in the representation of situations or the relay of experience, but rather in the revelation or production of novel views on the world *by* providing opportunity to reflect on the *conditions* of experience. He is arguing that aesthetic validity is an independent form of validity because it does not, as Wellmer argues, rely at all on truth-effects, rather only on the (an artwork's) capacity to engender new *ways of looking at the world*. Here Seel is again, as in *AD*, arguing for the reorienting function of art as its peculiar function. As indicated above, I see a problem in Seel's argument, which is the following: Seel essentially wins the independence of aesthetic validity at the cost of making it nonpractical. Clearly the initiation of processes of acquiring new ways of looking at the world itself has practical consequences.

What Seel ultimately fails to explain is how he proposes to keep aesthetic validity autonomous from other dimensions of validity when aesthetic validity is a function, as he correctly argues, of the capacity to articulate novel views on the world. He cannot uphold this autonomy for the following reasons: that a form of validity is a *fundamental* form of validity presupposes that claims with regard to that kind of validity are redeemed through different *means*. Habermas argues this by pointing out how truth claims are redeemed through theoretical argumentation or empirical demonstration, rightness claims are redeemed through moral argumentation, and truthfulness claims are redeemed through the consistency of action with speech. How will Seel describe the peculiarity of aesthetic validity? He does so by indicating that aesthetic validity can manifest itself *outside* of validity claims; this is one of two manifestations of aesthetic validity in his account:

1. This first form of aesthetic validity is evident in the *actuality* of a reorientation in the recipient of an aesthetic artifact through that aesthetic artifact. The problem here is that this validity is limited to social currency (*Geltung*) to the exclusion of validity (*Gültigkeit*). Such a form of validity contributes little to a theory of aesthetic *rationality,* because, alone, it represents, so to speak, the raising and redemption of a validity "claim" in one, *without* the possibility of contestation.

2. The other form of aesthetic validity that Seel's account includes, the one instantiated in the raising and contestation of explicit or implicit validity *claims,* will also not give him the autonomy for aesthetic validity that he is looking for: this is so because the *demonstration,* through aesthetic critique, of aesthetic "success" is parasitic on claims of nonaesthetic forms of validity. Aesthetic critique demonstrates not merely or primarily the *successful imparting* of view on the world to the recipient, but rather demonstrates the aesthetic artifact's *enabling the finding* of a view on the world. Here Seel's argument is sound. But clearly this demonstration through aesthetic critique is going to rely on all kinds of nonaesthetic validity claims (theoretical, empirical, practical, etc), as Seel himself indicates in *AD*.

That aesthetic critique is *parasitic* on claims of nonaesthetic forms of validity, on the one hand, and that the *actuality* of orientation-altering effects does not alone provide an adequate basis for an independent form of (aesthetic) rationality on the other hand, are my reasons for rejecting Seel's thesis that aesthetic validity, and, by extension, truth in art, is a nonderived form of validity. Furthermore, Seel cannot consistently hold both: (a) that aesthetic practice reorients the recipients of aesthetic artifacts in their view of the world, a reorientation that is irreducible to theoretical-instrumental, moral-practical, and subjective-preferential ways of relating to the world, or any combination thereof; *and* (b) that aesthetic experience is *not* a unifying form of experience. The perceptual reorientation that results from aesthetic experience can be a *unifying* form of experience to the extent that it turns on all of the ways of relating to the world. This understanding of the reorientation attained through aesthetic experience need not claim a *superior* form of knowledge (or emphatic form of truth) to be gained through aesthetic practice. This is so because the articulation of a way of looking at the world need not at all presuppose or implicitly claim that the view presented is the only or the only correct way of looking at the world. This may be the case under given circumstances, but the *primary* operation of the aesthetic articulation of a way of looking at the world is the presentation of a view that is *relevant* to the historical moment in which it is articulated, and that this relevance had been previously either unrecognized or underestimated.

The above discussion reveals a further, strange inconsistency within Seel's account. Seel's critique of Wellmer insisted that the validity of art be understood to be independent of truth-effects. At the same time, however, the very distinction with which Seel wants to ground the independence of aesthetic validity (*Geltung* outside of validity claims) implies that the validity of art depends on its performative effectiveness in orienting the recipient. Seel can only get out of this incoherence by maintaining, as he does, that the reorientation in the recipient attained through the reception and explication of aesthetic artifacts, is *purely projective* in nature, i.e. nonpractical in its immediate context. Thus, in a strange collusion with and indeed accentuation of Habermas's account, where only *certain* forms of perlocutionary effects are excluded from the (aesthetically) legitimate effects of aesthetic practice (see 3.1.2.2), Seel limits the legitimacy of aesthetic "effects" to perception and excludes all "practical" effects. Seel is right to point out that one can talk about whether and to what extent someone is reoriented in their way of looking at the world without asking whether that view is *right* or not, for instance. But to the extent that such a reorientation has potential subsequent effects in the world implies that aesthetic validity must be evaluated at least in part by those effects, *if* one understands the *actuality* of reorientation in worldview to be a measure of aesthetic validity, as Seel does. To limit aesthetic validity to this, however, turns aesthetic validity into mere facticity, and aesthetic rationality into a form of strategic reason on the production side of aesthetic practice, and into an evaluation of the efficiency of this strategic reason on the side of aesthetic criticism.

With Seel, I argue for the understanding of aesthetic validity as (in part) the validity of innovative worldview-articulation, but against Seel I argue that the notion of aesthetic validity is not fully captured by the reorienting or worldview-articulating capacity of art. In the last section of this chapter (3.3), I counter that, particularly in literature, due to the latter's linguistic medium, the validity of art (as literature) is in fact inseparable from its potential truth-effects. By this I mean to say that literary validity, and the literary rationality which turns on it, should be described in terms of the production of historically relevant views on the world, the subsequent "re-orientation" of literature's recipients, *and* the recipients' rational coordination of subsequent actions outside of the literary sphere. In the context of literary practice, Seel's critique of aesthetic rationality has the merit, among others, of debunking the notion that validity manifests itself only through (explicit) validity claims. But unlike Seel, I do not want to see aesthetic validity as comprised in part of the mere fact that certain artworks reorient their recipients with regard to their view on the world. Rather I want demonstrate *implicit validity claims* in the literary institution and its practices that determine the range of truth-effects at stake in the operation of literary rationality. But before elaborating on the concept of *literary* rationality, I will briefly revisit in the following subsection (3.2.4) the central theoretical problem mentioned at the beginning of this section (3.2): the relation between aesthetic and nonaesthetic forms of validity on the one hand, and the relation between aesthetic and nonaesthetic forms of rationality, on the other hand.

3.2.4 Aesthetic Validity and Aesthetic Rationality

Above I have given reasons for contending that none of the responses to Habermas's theory of communicative action from the perspective of aesthetic theory (Koppe, Wellmer, or Seel) alone presents an *adequate* and *coherent* account of the relation between aesthetic and nonaesthetic forms of validity on the one hand and between aesthetic rationality and nonaesthetic forms of rationality on the other hand. I have also indicated what aspects of each account contribute to my own account of aesthetic validity and aesthetic rationality. Here I want to briefly summarize what my argument has gained from the above discussion and offer my own account of aesthetic validity and aesthetic rationality.

Koppe correctly understands the articulation of subjective needs through aesthetic artifacts as inherently intersubjective, but ultimately adheres to Habermas's reduction of aesthetic rationality to expressive rationality. Koppe does this by locating the peculiarity of aesthetic rationality in a purportedly superior articulation of subjective needs (as compared to propositional or normative uses of language). Although belonging to expressive rationality, aesthetic practice furthermore embodies for Koppe an emphatic form thereof that renders it superior to "everyday" expressive speech acts (*Erlebnissätze*). But Koppe clearly wants the articulation of subjective needs in aesthetic practice to transcend the situation of the articulating subject: hence the *para-digmatic* (representative and exemplary) nature of the complexes of experience relayed through aesthetic practice. Once we no longer restrict the domain of aesthetic rationality to the expression of subjective experience in this way, however, it is no longer necessary to assert a *superiority* of aesthetic language in order to define its peculiarity, as Koppe does. Koppe's talk of the paradigmatic nature of the experience relayed through aesthetic practice is on the mark; but he does not draw the theoretical consequences from this argument for a comprehensive account of aesthetic validity.

Although he acknowledges the reliance of portrayals of paradigmatic experience on *truth claims,* the *normative* content of an articulation that lays claim to presenting paradigmatic experience, receives no attention at all in Koppe's account. It is not only the case that the claim to portray paradigmatic experience can be contested on the basis of facts and states of affairs (i.e. by challenging its attendant truth claims). It is also the case that such a claim can be challenged on moral grounds (i.e. by challenging its attendant normative claims). Such a contestation (or endorsement) could address the question whether the paradigmatic experience portrayed serves moral or political ends that are acceptable or objectionable (e.g., whether it brings to light the shared experience of a marginalized or disadvantaged social group, for instance, or, alternately, whether it tacitly legitimizes oppressive social structures). In other words, in addition to being evaluated according its *faithfully* representing a complex of subjective experience, a portrayal of paradigmatic experience can evaluated on the basis of both its *accuracy* and *appropriateness* in a given socio-historical context. For this reason I argue that the *interrelation* between the three fundamental forms of validity is constitutive of the aesthetic validity claim. I indicated above that understanding aesthetic validity claims as containing subsidiary validity claims of all the types that Habermas identifies lets one see the peculiarity of literary language as consisting in its capacity to articulate *ways of looking at* the objective, social, and subjective worlds *in light of* shareable subjective experiences. In this sense Koppe's account does not adequately describe the claim of aesthetic validity, because it makes aesthetic rationality into an expressive rationality that avails itself only of truthfulness (and truth) claims.

Wellmer's argument for "truth" in art as a phenomenon of interference between the different dimensions of validity suggests the kind of interrelation between the three fundamental forms of validity that is missing in Koppe's account. Wellmer argues that whereas the three fundamental forms of validity interfere in aesthetic validity claims, the latter are not reducible to any of the former or any combination thereof. By rejecting reductionist accounts of aesthetic validity, Wellmer clears the way for a distinct form of aesthetic *rationality,* one that operates in relative independence from the three basic forms of rationality in Habermas's account. This relative independence was not yet clearly articulated in Koppe, where aesthetic rationality is cashed out in terms of expressive rationality.

Wellmer's thesis of aesthetic validity as an interference phenomenon follows a correct intuition, but he does not fully specify what he means by *interference* of validity forms, and therefore does not offer a descriptively complete account of the peculiarity of aesthetic rationality. If Wellmer holds that aesthetic validity constitutes a phenomenon of interference in the *strong sense* that the validity claims raised through the presentation of aesthetic artifacts conflict with or even contradict one another, then he is describing only a subset of aesthetic practice. The literary use of irony, for instance, could be described in terms of a conflict between a truthfulness claim and a truth claim, respectively: an author says the opposite of what she means, and if what she means is successfully relayed, it was only so relayed by virtue of the strategic deployment of a (false) truth claim. There is no reason to assume, however, that the validity of aesthetic artifacts *as aesthetic artifacts* lies wholly in the playful deployment of contradictory or at least opposed validity claims, even if such a strategy is characteristic for many aesthetic artifacts. One can equally imagine cases where an artwork work that is considered aesthetically valid is not structured around such contradictions.

I want to argue that aesthetic validity constitutes a phenomenon of interference between other forms of validity primarily in the *weak sense* that the negotiation of aesthetic validity claims (potentially) effects the reorientation of the recipients of aesthetic artifacts *with regard* to complexes of experience in which descriptive, normative, and expressive forms of validity are indistinct. That is, aesthetic validity is not, as Wellmer argues, *itself* a phenomenon of interference between validity forms; rather, the aesthetically valid artwork itself articulates and through doing so gives rise to experiences in which validity forms interfere. Aesthetic experience, i.e. experimentation with one's own experience by experiencing another experience, consists in the reevaluation of previous patterns of expectation and behavior. This reevaluation is made possible through the gaining of a novel perspective on the objective, social, and subjective worlds, and therefore involves taking a critical stance toward certain aspects of those worlds (more exactly, toward the validity of prior assumptions about those aspects). Aesthetic *critique* aims to make out, and in some form reject or endorse, the various views on the world taken up by the artwork. Its methods and techniques are various, and I do not argue that they invariably serve one end. I do hold, however, that the particular form of *rationality* that motivates the production, reception, and critique of aesthetic artifacts, operates *primarily* with an eye to a form of validity in which all the dimensions of the everyday notion of truth (truth, rightness, and truthfulness) commingle: authenticity. The question of whether and in what way a portrayal of a shareable experience is *authentic,* is the question peculiar to the aesthetic form of rationality.

Seel aptly argues for the understanding of aesthetic validity as the validity of innovative articulation of ways-the-world-is. Seel points out, in contradistinction to Wellmer, that the specificity of the aesthetic form of validity does not lie in *world-disclosure,* but rather in the *disclosure of world-disclosure,* by which he means the opening up of *ways of looking at the world.* Attempting to clear up Wellmer's thesis of aesthetic validity as a phenomenon of interference between nonaesthetic dimensions of validity, Seel gives a more convincing account of how it is that aesthetic validity actually extends to involve all the dimensions of the everyday notion of validity. The basic structure of Seel's argument could be reconstructed as follows: An argument for the aesthetic validity of a piece of literature, for instance, relies on a demonstration of the "successful" articulation of an experience. *What* is validated by the positive critical appraisal of a piece of literature is a "way of looking at the world" gained through *having an experience*. *Having an experience* means a calling into question and subsequent (1) alteration (loss or accentuation) of a previously accepted "way of looking at the world"; or (2) gain of a new "way of looking at the world." A "way of looking at the world" encompasses relations to the social, objective, and subjective worlds. An *articulation of an experience* is successful only if it makes the context of meaningfulness of a particular situation *present* to the recipient and in turn initiates (or could initiate) an experience on the part of the recipient. The experience initiated by a successful articulation of another experience is an *aesthetic experience*. The work performed by an aesthetic experience is therefore the gain, loss, or accentuation of a "way of looking at the world." And because a "way of looking at the world" involves all three "worlds" (i.e. objective, social, subjective), aesthetic validity is a function of all the forms of validity on which claims with regard to these worlds turn (truth, rightness, and truthfulness). To the extent that it clarifies how it is that aesthetic validity claims reference subsidiary, nonaesthetic validity claims, Seel's account is quite useful for my argument.

But Seel, and here he incorrectly diverges from Wellmer, is content to leave the *redemption* of claims of aesthetic validity at the success of the performative articulation of a novel way of looking at the world, i.e. the *presentation* of a view on the world through an artifact that effects the *adoption* of a new view on the world on the part of the recipient of that artifact. Against Seel I argue that the notion of aesthetic validity is not fully captured by the reorienting or worldview-articulating capacity of art. I do *not* argue, however, that the claim of aesthetic validity is redeemed in full only when its potential truth-effects are realized, but rather that the claim of aesthetic validity contains irreducibly normative and assertory elements. That is, the negotiation (i.e. the raising, contestation, and endorsement or rejection) of the authenticity claim consists in some form or another, in the negotiation of claims of all of the three fundamental forms of validity. And aesthetic rationality does not per se give justificatory priority to any one of these kinds of validity claims. Aesthetic critique, for instance, can challenge the *accuracy* of a portrayal (i.e. its reflection of facts and states of affairs), but for such a contestation of a truth claim to be an aesthetic one, that critique must also give reasons why the "inaccurate" reflection of reality is also *disgenuine* and *unjustifiable*, i.e. why it does not redeem its own truthfulness and rightness claims.

Because aesthetic rationality is primarily concerned with giving reasons for or against the authenticity of a portrayal of shared experience, I argue, it a priori bears on issues of generalizable concern. This means that the operation of aesthetic rationality does not merely put forth ways of *looking* at the world, and furthermore that an artwork is not aesthetically valid merely on the basis of its successful reorientation of its recipients. The operation of aesthetic rationality also, through its reorienting effects, puts forth ways of *acting* in the world. I do not argue that the redemption of the claim of aesthetic validity of an artwork depends on its part in the coordination of any particular actions, but rather on the consequences for subsequent actions that the reorientation of a recipient of an artwork has or could have. Whereas the claim of aesthetic validity may not be explicit in the artwork in question, the fact of that artwork's public appearance and its public discussion imply that it is treated as raising a validity claim, one that is substantiated (or not), on the basis of the artwork and the complex of views on the objective, social, and (respective) subjective worlds that it articulates. The raising and contestation of this complex claim of authenticity, and its endorsement or rejection, by means of arguments, are the fundamental functions of aesthetic rationality. That aesthetic argumentation thus relies of theoretical and practical forms of argumentation and not merely, as Habermas argues, on the demonstration of expressive truthfulness or untruthfulness, means that aesthetic rationality performs a fundamentally public function. This is particularly evident in the realm of verbal aesthetic practice. For this reason I elaborate, in the following section, on the notion of a specifically *literary* form of aesthetic rationality in order to subsequently make the argument for the necessity of the function fulfilled by the literary public sphere, and the operation of literary rationality in the public sphere at large.

3.3 LITERARY RATIONALITY

In this section I give an account of the peculiar nature of literary rationality. In the previous sections (3.1–3.2), I defined aesthetic rationality as the form of rationality at work in practices and discourses that are fundamentally concerned with the complex claim of authenticity. I argued against Habermas that authenticity claims are not raised and disputed merely on the basis of a claim of expressive validity (truthfulness). Rather, I argued, the claim of authenticity contains irreducibly descriptive and normative aspects, and the authenticity claim is indeed intersubjectively contestable (i.e. can be endorsed or rejected with the help of theoretical, empirical, and moral-practical arguments, contrary to what Habermas argues). When one raises an authenticity claim by presenting an aesthetic artifact to the public, one claims, in addition to at least implicitly claiming to present a transparent portrayal of *subjective* experiences, to *represent* in two further senses of that term (*repräsentieren* and *vertreten*): (1) to accurately portray certain (relevant) objective states of affairs, and (2) to articulate a shared or shareable (paradigmatic) experience of objective or subjective states of affairs. This was my basic account of the authenticity claim at work in aesthetic rationality. This section adds to that basic account in two ways: by defining the literary form of aesthetic rationality specifically (in 3.3.1); by defining the peculiar public function of literary rationality (in 3.3.2); and by establishing a key method of transporting intersubjectively shareable, authentic experience through concrete literary means, namely through the use of *allegory* (in 3.3.3).

3.3.1   Literary Rationality as a Peculiar Form of Aesthetic Rationality

What distinguishes the literary variety of aesthetic rationality from non-literary varieties thereof is, trivially, the (communicative) use of language (as compared to the nonlinguistic systems of signification in painting and music, for instance). This state of affairs makes literature a clear candidate for qualifying as a forum for communicative action for Habermas. As the discussion up to this point has demonstrated, however, Habermas gives a reductive account of aesthetic, and hence literary rationality as a form of expressive rationality. Yet Habermas mentions although does not elaborate on a criterion that would yield a more complex account of aesthetic rationality. In his general description of aesthetic validity Habermas includes, in addition to the exemplarity of experience and the preferability of cultural value standards discussed above (see 3.1.2.1), the criterion of *well-formedness*.

This criterion refers, unlike the exemplarity of the experience portrayed and the preferability of cultural value standards posited through it, exclusively to the *formal qualities* of an aesthetic artifact. *Any* use of language can be evaluated according to its well-formedness. This evaluation is separate from a critique of the particular descriptive, normative, and truthfulness validity claims raised by a use of language. In the case of distinguishing the literary form of rationality from nonliterary forms of aesthetic rationality, the criterion of well-formedness is particularly productive because well-formedness is not a determinate concept. Concerning the use of language, one can distinguish two different kinds of well-formedness: linguistic and literary. In nonlinguistic forms of aesthetic practice, numerous other elements, such as balance, dynamic range, etc. make up the criteria according to which aesthetic well-formedness is evaluated. I argue that well-formedness has, in the case of the literary use of language, a different status than in either nonliterary aesthetic critique or the evaluation of a use of language according to standards of mere linguistic well-formedness, precisely because of the peculiar kind of language use in question. Linguistic well-formedness, for instance, which is a necessary condition for the comprehension of a standard speech act, is neither a necessary nor a sufficient condition for qualifying as literarily well-formed: often enough the literarily well-formed is, according to traditional norms, linguistically "ill-formed." Neologisms and fragmentary sentence structure are only two examples of this. Of course, these can and often do occur in nonliterary uses of language as well, but my point is that whereas adherence to or legitimizable deviation from traditional grammatical rules is a sufficient criterion for evaluating the well-formedness of an everyday use of language, it is *not* a sufficient criterion for evaluating the well-formedness of a literary artifact.

What ultimately distinguishes literary from nonliterary uses of language, and hence literary from mere linguistic well-formedness, is, not remarkably, the same characteristic that renders literary rationality a form of aesthetic rationality: the justificatory priority of the authenticity claim. What makes literary rationality *distinct* from nonliterary forms of aesthetic rationality, is moreover not merely its medium (language) but what it conveys *about* its medium. The communicative use of language in an aesthetic form (i.e. with an authenticity claim attached to it) is a peculiar use of language not merely because it discloses issues of generalizable concern (shareable experiences), which various forms of theoretical or practical discourse can do equally well. And the communicative use of language in an aesthetic form is distinct also not merely because it discloses ways of *looking at* issues of generalizable concern. Rather, the communicative use of language in an aesthetic form is a peculiar use of language because it discloses *novel ways of articulating, through language use, issues of generalizable concern.* This is the insight about the specific nature of literary rationality that runs in some form through all of the accounts of aesthetic rationality that I have discussed so far, although I have not found it formulated anywhere in this way. This insight clearly also provides the link to the discussion of the peculiar function of literary rationality in the public sphere that is carried out in the following subsection. Before turning to that argument, however, I will briefly revisit certain aspects of Habermas's account of literary rationality as read out of his discussion of the "poetic function" of language.

Above I have argued that Habermas's account of literary rationality is inadequate. In that part of my argument I focused primarily on the reduction of aesthetic rationality to expressive rationality. But I view the account to be inaccurate also to the extent that literature is assigned the role of pure world-disclosure, a trait that would otherwise seem positive enough. The literary institution is distinct as a cultural system of action for Habermas due to the peculiarity of the poetic function that is fore-grounded in the literary use of language: "The literature industry [as a cultural system of action] administers capacities of world-disclosure."[133] The flipside of Habermas's characterization of the poetic function as world-disclosure in its pure form is the predominance of rhetoric at the expense of argumentation:

> What constitutes the *priority* and the structure-forming power of the poetic function is, namely, not the deviation of a fictional representation from a documentary account of a process, but rather an exemplary treatment, which separates the event from its context and makes it into

an innovative, world-opening, eye-opening representation, whereby the rhetorical media of the representation step outside of communicative routines and take on a life of their own.[134]

Habermas's aim in the cited article is to defend the genre-distinction between literary criticism and philosophy against the likes of Derrida, who reduces all communication-oriented language use to so much rhetorical strategy. As mentioned above, Habermas's argument has its valid and contestable points in this regard, and I cannot address them all here. I want only to refer to Habermas's comments on the fundamental character of the literary as compared to the philosophical use of language. Habermas concedes that philosophy, just as literary criticism, cannot but avail itself of rhetorical techniques in order to get its point across. In this sense, the two, literary criticism and philosophy, are related. But here is also where the comparison ends, on Habermas's account, because each uses a different form of argumentation. This is certainly accurate: the entire preceding discussion has tried to show how aesthetic rationality relates to but is distinct from other forms of rationality due, in part, to the variety of its modes of argumentation. The problem that I see in Habermas's account here is the seeming conflation of literature and literary criticism. When Habermas argues that literature cannot solve problems because it is fundamentally rhetorical,[135] he seems again to be operating with an understanding of literature that sees literary aesthetic practice as autonomous, as he does in *TCA* (see above discussion in 3.1.2.1).

Admittedly, Habermas does specify in later essays that although the suspension of illocutionary force is characteristic of literary *work,* the *presentation* of a literary work does have an illocutionary aspect. This is what allows literary criticism to serve a translating, mediating function: from the experience articulated in the literary work into everyday language, essentially. Because Habermas sees such a bridging function, however, it is odd that he does not consider literary production and literary criticism as belonging to one, literary, institution. How does he propose getting from the suspension of illocutionary force in literature itself to the communicative practice of literary criticism? Is the actual communicative potential of literature fully reliant on interpretive interventions on the part of literary critics?

I maintain, in contrast to Habermas, that in order to fully account for the communicative potential of the literary use of language, it is necessary to consider the institutional framework that embraces both literature and literary criticism. This institution is held together by common presuppositions about what it is that is at stake in the presentation of literature and the business of literary criticism. This is another way of saying that literature and literary criticism are determined by a common concern for a particular kind of illocution. This illocution consists in the at least implicit claim of literary practice to occasion a discussion of what constitutes an adequate and elegant (i.e. authentic) presentation of historically-relevant complexes of shareable experience.

3.3.2   Literary Rationality in the Public Sphere

The above discussion of the nature of aesthetic rationality and of the peculiarity of the literary form thereof has been carried out, as indicated in the introductory chapter (see 1.2), in order to provide a basis for supporting the argument that, by means of their own form of rationality, *literature and literary discourse uniquely invigorate public discussion*. Literature can do this, by producing a rationally grounded *resonance* in a reading/listening public, which can result, on the basis of the complex claim of authenticity that is internal to the literary institution and negotiable on the basis of the descriptive, normative, and expressive content of a given text and its presentation, in a *practically consequential reorientation* in the recipients' view on the world. This is why the "private" reception of literature, and not just literary discourse, as Habermas argues, belongs in a sense to the public sphere. The described reorientation is not merely a matter of a novel *perception* of the world through experiencing another (aesthetically articulated) experience on the part of the recipient of the literary artifact, but also his acquisition of novel means of articulating, through language, his own experience. Herein lies the *practical* necessity of the literary public sphere's *function,* not the necessity of literature, in the public sphere at large.

My argument for this practical necessity of the function of literary rationality in the public sphere at large runs like this: whereas literature's relation to the public sphere is not merely one of historical priority, and conversely, whereas literary culture itself is not a requirement of a well-functioning public sphere, literary culture does fill a capacity necessary to the well-functioning public sphere: the communicative use of language in an aesthetic form. This argument is weaker than it may first seem: I do not want to argue that any well-functioning public sphere must include a literary public sphere, but rather that the *function* that literature serves in the public sphere is a *practically* necessary component of the well-functioning public sphere.

It would be helpful to first clarify the nature of this argument and compare it to other kinds of arguments that can be made in this context. There are four kinds of arguments that one can make in order to establish the necessity of the literary public sphere, or, alternately, of the necessity of the *function* that literary culture serves, for the well-functioning public sphere at large:

- the literary public sphere is a *conceptually necessary* component of the public sphere at large;
- the *function* that the literary public serves (has traditionally served) is a conceptually necessary component of the public sphere at large;

- the literary public sphere is a *practically* "necessary" component of the public sphere at large;
- the *function* that the literary public sphere serves (has traditionally served) is a practically "necessary" component of the public sphere at large.

The first two, stronger arguments are *a priori* arguments, and endorse the following views, respectively:

1. one has to assume a literary public in order to imagine a public sphere at all; or
2. one has to assume an institution that fulfills the function that the literary public fulfills (has traditionally fulfilled), in order to imagine a public sphere at all.

The last two, weaker arguments, are *effectiveness* or *preferability* arguments,[136] and endorse the following views, respectively:

3. for a public sphere to function well in practice, a literary public sphere must/should at least aid in the public articulation of matters of general concern; and
4. for a public sphere to function well in practice, an institution that fulfills the function that the literary public sphere fulfills (has traditionally fulfilled), must/should at least aid in the public articulation of matters of general concern.

Whether arguments 3 and 4 are effectiveness or, alternately, preferability arguments depends on whether one relies on a *description* of literature's peculiar and exceptional capacity for articulation of matters of general concern (effectiveness argument), or, alternately, on an ultimately subjectively grounded *endorsement* of literature's mode of articulating matters of general concern (preferability argument). My overall argument corresponds to number 4, and will rely on a description of literature's peculiar and exceptional capacity for public articulation of matters of general concern. Hence, I argue for the better, i.e. more effective, functioning of a public sphere that includes an institution that serves the function that the literary public serves (has traditionally served).

How can one demonstrate this greater effectiveness? Faced with the general problem of demonstrating the singular relationship between literature and the public sphere, it clearly will not help to focus on the function that literature *shares* with other segments of the public sphere: the rationally motivated articulation of matters of general(izable) concern. Indeed, if this were a sufficient condition for a well-functioning public sphere, one can imagine a society with a well-functioning public sphere in which there is no literature in its traditional form at all. Along this line, one could argue that there are numerous means available for the rationally motivated articulation of matters of public concern. Showing this counters the strong arguments 1 and 3 above, both of which untenably make literature's *contingent* contribution to the public sphere a *necessary* component of the public sphere. The fact that literature has traditionally provided an important channel of public communication does not alone substantiate the claim that literature itself is a necessary component of a well-functioning public sphere. That is, there is no necessary connection at all between the rationally motivated articulation of matters of general concern and the literary medium itself. This means not only that the role that literature played in the formation of the public sphere was a historically contingent one, but also that it could be substituted *in its function* in the public sphere, to the extent that literature is understood as one form among others of the rationally motivated articulation of matters of general concern.

But this is only one part of literature's function within the public sphere, I argue. One could try to establish the effectiveness claim I raised above by identifying a peculiar function that extends beyond this basic function, by arguing for the *uniqueness* of literature's contribution to the public sphere. But establishing the uniqueness, i.e. the peculiar capacity to invigorate public discussion that I claimed for the literary public sphere earlier on, will also not *alone* establish the practical necessity of the literary public sphere's function in the public sphere at large, *if* literature's uniqueness is understood as consisting in its competence in *thematizing* complex issues of public concern. A good uniqueness argument will have to go beyond an understanding of the literary articulation of matters of generalizable concern as particularly *productive* with regard to the number and variety of issues it raises. Rather, it would have to show how literature can *qualitatively* improve public discussion, and could go as follows: It is plausible to claim that the institution of literature makes a contribution to the public sphere that could not be sufficiently substituted by the contributions of other institutions of public self-reflection, such as those of the social sciences or nonliterary forms of aesthetic practice. The uniqueness of this contribution lies in its combination of the linguistic medium and aesthetic form; neither the social sciences nor nonliterary forms of aesthetic practice (nor any other institution) combines these.[137] In order for the uniqueness argument to establish the greater effectiveness, i.e. the better functioning, of the public sphere that contains a literary public sphere, one would have to show, as I intend to, that the use of language in aesthetic form (which is the aspect that extends its function beyond that of a thematizing agent), *enriches* public discussion, and does so not by disclosing issues alone, but rather by disclosing *ways of looking at* issues.

Demonstrating this greater effectiveness is not sufficient for establishing the necessity of literature as such for the well-functioning public sphere. As indicated above, however, I argue not that a well-functioning public sphere must include a literary public sphere per se, but rather that in any well-functioning public sphere the *function* that literary culture serves (has traditionally served) is served (by some institution). This is different than argument 2 above, which holds that the function that the literary public serves is a *conceptually* necessary component of the public sphere at large. That is, I do not even want argue that one has to assume an institution that fulfills the function that the literary public fulfills (has traditionally fulfilled), in order to imagine a public sphere *at all*. Indeed, one can imagine a public sphere in which aesthetic form is not a concern at all, i.e. where the authenticity claim is not raised and disputed, but rather only the three fundamental forms of validity claims that Habermas describes in *TCA*. In particular, the unrestricted raising and contestation of descriptive and normative validity claims alone promises to satisfy the conditions of the public sphere as Habermas understands it: the rational articulation and negotiation of matters of generalizable concern among (at least formally) equal discourse participants.

Even the addition of the truthfulness claim does not sufficiently animate this bare-bones picture of the public sphere, however. I argue that the authenticity claim, which contains, but is not reducible to either of these three dimensions of validity (or any combination of them), uniquely invigorates public discussion. Literature, in particular, can do this by producing a rationally grounded *resonance* in a reading/listening public, which can result, on the basis of the complex claim of authenticity internal to the literary institution, in the *reorientation* in the recipients' view of the world. Herein lies the *practical* necessity of the literary public sphere's function in the public sphere at large. This is neither an argument for a strong, conceptual necessity, nor a merely prescriptive, preferability argument. Rather, it is an effectiveness argument, which, in order to work, must describe the exceptional capacity of literature to articulate *ways of considering matters of generalizable concern*. Giving such an account of the peculiarity of literary rationality is the goal that a Habermasian social philosophy of literature sets itself.

The above argument concerning the necessity of the function of the literary public sphere is, as mentioned above, meant neither as an argument for a strong, conceptual necessity, nor a merely prescriptive, preferability argument with regard to literature's role in the public sphere. The kind of argument needed in order to establish the practical necessity of the function of the literary public sphere in the public sphere at large is one that shows how literature can *qualitatively* improve, and not just quantitatively augment, public discussion, that is, how it *enriches* public discussion by making a contribution that is not made by other parts of the public sphere. This kind of effectiveness thesis is presented in the above account of literary rationality: the public sphere in which—on the basis of experiences that can intersubjectively be attributed authenticity—not merely issues of generalizable concern, but also the validity of ways of looking at and articulating such issues is negotiated, is a more effective, i.e. better functioning, public sphere than one in which such experiences are not reflexively experienced and publicly articulated. Indeed, this is the kind of effectiveness argument that is ultimately implied by Habermas's claim that moral-practical discourse occasionally must rely on the "creative process of semantization which unleashes potential for new meanings via the nonpropositional symbolic systems of literature, art and music:"[138] the processes of needs interpretation that literary practice, as an aesthetic practice, performs, revitalizes, and improves public discussion by not merely *expressing* situations of need, but by redefining what counts as a situation of need, an authentic articulation of shareable experience, and so on.

The effectiveness thesis concerning the role of the literary public sphere in the public sphere at large would ultimately have to be demonstrated by means of a thorough empirical analysis of literary practices, a demonstration which I can approach only very incompletely here. In order to make the effectiveness argument *plausible,* I turn to a brief analysis of a novel and its public discussion in the particular socio-historical context of post-unification Germany. Because my analysis focuses on the novel and its published reception, it cannot and does not intend to warrant conclusions concerning the specific reading experiences of its audience. Instead, my analysis aims at an account of (1) the *author's approach* to rendering a particular complex of subjective experiences; and (2) the *mode of evaluating* the success of the author's attempt as read out of the published discussion of the novel. Not only does the second of these, the study of the texts' reception, support the above argument for the unique role of literary practice in the literary public sphere: also the text itself, in particular through its attempt allegorically to represent shareable complexes, is an engagement with the political public sphere. Both the specific text in question and its reception are indicative of a concern for the intersubjectively authentic portrayal of complexes of experience that is characteristic of literature in general, a *fundamental* orientation in literary rationality that becomes particularly evident, I argue, in light of the *specific* historical circumstances of post-unification Germany.

3.3.3   Authenticity and Allegory: Categories of Literary Rationality

Before turning to the text in question, I will indicate how some of the key theoretical concepts discussed above apply to the analysis of their literary texts. First, several related but distinct notions of authenticity must be differentiated from one another. *Authenticity* can be taken, most broadly, to signify the distinguishing feature of an "accurate" representation of subjective experience. In this least restrictive definition of the term, authenticity is a form of truthfulness, as "being true to oneself" in one's representations of oneself. This sense of the term reveals a possible, but not necessary connection to an emphatic notion of subjectivity, according to which the standard by which the "accuracy" of self-representations is to be measured is none other than the subject engaged in the self-representation in question. From the perspective of the writing author, though, the notion of authenticity is often enough not reducible to merely successful, factually "accurate" self-representation, but rather is fundamentally understood in terms of an establishment of identity through the act of writing. Literary critics also frequently focus on this meaning of authenticity, the sort manifest in the "active" formation of identity through strategic self-revelation. But part of the interest in evaluating the authenticity of a piece of literature in this sense, I argue, lies in determining its capacity to capture a shareable feature of the experience in question, or, effectively the same, to render the articulation of this feature of experience in a particularly elegant manner. The latter is the same as saying that the experience of many is captured in the portrayal of the experience of the one. This is a statement, in skeletal form, of what I mean to designate with the notion of intersubjective authenticity.

This weakest, least restrictive, sense of *authenticity,* looks a lot like Habermas's concept of truthfulness, according to which a validity claim of the truthfulness cannot be corroborated through demonstration or theoretical argument as could a truth or rightness claim, but rather the sense of which is fundamentally bound up with the collective attribution of truthfulness, believability, credibility, etc., to a speaker or writer on the part of his/her audience. This weakest sense of *authenticity* also touches, at least peripherally, on the factually accurate representation of the objective world (verifiable objects and states of affairs), at least insofar as the latter is relevant to an articulation of one's own complexes of experiences.

But it is not the case that autobiographies are the only works to which authenticity is attributed. Rather, more important to the concept of authenticity in the literary context, and what renders it somewhat more restrictive than the weakest formulation of *authenticity* above, is, specifically, the concern for the fittingness of allegories. Regard for this concept of authenticity is focused, more generally, on the existence, nature, and extent of allegories, or at least allegorical or other comparative elements in the text in question, a mode of literary inquiry that will become particularly relevant in the text in question. This concern with allegorical elements further reflects the fact that the determination of the "accuracy" of a self-representation is an approximating endeavor. It is approximate because the assessment of authenticity is not primarily concerned with describing an account of one's own experience in terms of a single meaning, but has, rather, to do with disclosing a richness of probable or at least potential meanings of a self-representation. It is self-evident that literary language itself and the language of literary criticism tends to stress polysemy, and indeed to reject those analyses of works of literature that more or less reduce a text to a single interpretation. Indeed, this mode of assessing the authenticity of literary texts is not fundamentally concerned with determining meanings at all, but rather with interpreting what Martin Seel called contexts of meaningfulness.[139]

A different and even more restrictive sense of authenticity is at work when the term is used to describe the author's freedom from involvement in social artifice. This notion of authenticity recurs frequently in discussions of the author of the text in question, Wolfgang Hilbig, as we shall see. An author whose texts are considered authentic in this sense is one who is in the position to articulate complexes of experience in a "natural" way because of his/her existence at the margins of society. This is, in other words, the commonly used outsider-argument, which identifies the source of the author's authenticity in his/her, resistance, conscious or not, to the homogenizing norms of society at large, and to the commodifying norms of the literature industry specifically. One finds reliance on such a notion all over in the reception of Hilbig, for instance. This resistance to artifice is often enough, although not necessarily, linked to class and social role, whereby the more mundane generally counts as the more "authentic."

A final sense of authenticity, and one the attribution of which to a text or its author is generally most limited among the senses of the term described here, concerns a text's elegance in capturing the specificity of a particular socio-historical situation. This is the sense of authenticity that most closely corresponds to the notion of intersubjective authenticity that I am introducing. This is so because the attribution of elegance implies an assumption of the applicability of the complex of experience in question to numerous other individuals. A literary work considered authentic in this strongest sense is considered so due to its rendering of a shareable experience through an account of a subjectively "specific" complex of experience. The strength of this kind of authenticity claim with regard to the scope of the applicability of the experience can vary. In the case of Hilbig, for instance, the author can be understood to render a paradigmatic account of the experience of East German authors or of East Germans in general in their adapting to radically changed life circumstances in unified Germany.

It should be pointed out that the weaker notion of authenticity outlined above, which, in the literary context, celebrates the richness of potential meanings through allegorical or other comparative elements in representations, stands, at least *prima facie*, in contradiction to the stronger sense just discussed. The focus on the specificity of a particular sociohistorical situation central to this last notion of authenticity runs against the tendency of authors and many critics to resist the reduction of the text to an interpretation that emphasizes the multiplicity of textual meanings. Often enough, as we shall see in the case of Hilbig, this resistance is coupled with a rejection of attempts to cull more or less clear normative claims, or, more specifically, political claims from a text. Ascertaining such claims of a text and its author is often seen by such literary critics and, when he or she gives voice to such objections, by the respective author, as challenging the autonomy of art, whether or not such terminology would be used.

What an author such as Hilbig, who, rightfully so, does not wish to be cast as a mere political commentator, and who, for this reason, resists political interpretations of his own texts, ultimately objects to in reductive political interpretations, is the unnecessary and, indeed, detrimental confusion of literary and practical rationality. The age-old notion defended here is that the validity of a literary work cannot be assessed merely on the basis of political claims that it may be deemed to raise. But neither can the assessment of the aesthetic merit of a piece of literature be made (nor is it, in fact) without a consideration of the normative claims that it raises. Any reading of a text with an eye to the latter's aesthetic qualities will necessarily also either address its normative claims or at least make tacit assumptions with regard to these, without thereby necessarily precluding the possibility of a multitude of valid readings. The point here is that presuming normative content in a published literary text relevant to the particular historical context of its own writing is not *eo ipso* a reduction of its semantic richness, especially to the extent that the text represents shareable complexes of experience through allegorical elements.

One further kind of preliminary distinction among types of authenticity claims must be made. Whereas assertions with regard to the authenticity of a text in criticism and scholarship tend to be made more or less explicit, with more or less thoroughgoing reasons given for the respective judgment, the claim of authenticity within the text may be more or less implicit. There are at least two senses in which such an implicit claim of authenticity can be raised by an author, by a text, or by an author through a text. First, some kind of validity claim is raised through the mere placement of a text into circulation in the public sphere. An author who claims to write only for him- or herself, a predilection common to many contemporary authors, will have a difficult time answering the question why he or she publishes his work at all, if not to engage in a more or less communicative practice, which, as such, is characterized by the negotiation of validity claims. If it can reasonably be established that what is generally and fundamentally at issue in a literary work is the paradigmatic nature of the complexes of experiences portrayed in it, then, it seems, it is also reasonable to conclude that a *claim* of authenticity is raised through the mere publication of a literary work. Whether that particular work actually embodies an authentic representation of experience is another question.

The second way in which a claim of authenticity can be raised implicitly is the extent to which it can be raised negatively, as is arguably the case in Hilbig's writings, that is to say, through the portrayal of inauthenticity. Or, more exactly, by portraying the barriers to forming a self-image with which one can live, i.e. barriers to an authentic sense of self. It has yet to be seen how this is a key way in which the selected text, in its own way, addresses the question of the possibility of authentic identity formation in post-unification Germany.

Central to this negotiation of authentic identity is the use of allegory as the medium for the representation of subjective complexes of experience as shareable. I understand *allegory* here not as a designation of genre, but rather as a way of reading texts. This approach to textual interpretation is occasioned not merely by the texts themselves and their figurative content, to whatever extent they may explicitly, internally reflect on their own allegorical elements. Allegorical readings are equally symptomatic of cultural conditions in which such texts are created. In the context of post-unification Germany, I argue, it is a need to find representations of subjective complexes of experience that can capture shareable aspects thereof that ultimately makes these texts into allegories, and, in turn, motivates their serving as bearers of an intersubjective exchange, as the focus of the public reflection on the intimate connections between personal memory and collective history.

4 The Claim of Authenticity

Wolfgang Hilbig and the Novel *"Ich"*

Wolfgang Hilbig's 1993 novel *"Ich"*[1] is particularly well suited for an illustration of my thesis concerning the authenticity claim and the workings of literary rationality for two reasons: on the one hand because the novel itself centers on (explicitly thematizes) the problem of the subjectivity and authentic identity, and on the other hand due to the novel's acclaim as an aesthetic success. The discussion of the novel would be aided by a brief consideration of Hilbig's biographical background and a short overview of the critical appraisal of Hilbig's oeuvre. For this purpose I will rely in the following on a comprehensive collection of autobiographical and critical essays on Hilbig.[2]

Hilbig was born in 1941 in Meuselwitz, a town in the brown-coal-mining region of Saxony-Thuringia located some 40 kilometers south of Leipzig. Born into a mining family, Hilbig was raised by his mother and maternal grandparents, his father having been reported missing in action near Stalingrad in 1942, never to return. Hilbig was a laborer in various industrial capacities in the German Democratic Republic (GDR) until 1980, always writing in secret on the side. The need for Hilbig to conceal his hobby had begun in his childhood: Hilbig's grandfather, an orphaned peasant from the Polish Ukraine who had never seen a school from the inside, viewed everything in print as deceitful nonsense. In 1978, some of Hilbig's poems were broadcast in the *Hessischer Rundfunk* in the Federal Republic of Germany (FRG), and subsequently he was able to publish his first poetry collection, *Abwesenheit*.[3] Hilbig had pursued this publication in West Germany without the permission of the East German authorities and was subsequently required to pay a substantial fine for his so-called "breach of exchange control regulations." Eventually, with the assistance of renowned East German authors, Hilbig was able to publish in East Germany and live as a freelance writer. But in 1985 the GDR authorities granted him a one-year exit visa, and Hilbig subsequently settled in the FRG. He successfully applied for an extension of the visa, which would have expired at a point in time when the GDR no longer formally existed.

In his numerous prose and lyrical publications, Hilbig developed a style that placed him, in the eyes of critics, in ranks with the unseeming literary pair Kafka and Hölderlin. Hilbig has been seen as the culmination of an antirealism represented by surrealism, dadaism, and concrete poetry. Literary scholar Uwe Wittstock characterizes Hilbig's works as "literary acts of sabotage against the foundations of our everyday sense of reality."[4] This corresponds to Hilbig's own literary self-understanding: realistic literature is for Hilbig a

> "completely secondary, if not tertiary thing. When we consider that reality is relatively superimposed on that which must be the universe, very relatively, and furthermore, that language is a medium that is superimposed on this reality," then whatever might come into being through the author's focus on this reality [literature] would "in fact be tertiary at best."[5]

The trope of the "unreality" of perceived reality runs straight through Hilbig's texts. Hilbig's protagonists (and antiheroes) are paradigms of uncertainty, never sure of their own thoughts. His texts are strung through with vocabulary that evokes an atmosphere of vagueness and approximation. The reader of Hilbig's texts is led to doubt the stability of the personality of his figures, just as the figures themselves doubt this stability. As Wittstock writes, Hilbig's figures "place themselves quasi in subjunctive, place their 'I' in quotation marks and thus also the stories that they report."[6] This dissolution of personality is thematically central, for instance, to the novel *"I,"* and the radical skepticism with regard to one's own personality is emblematized in the citation marks contained in its title. Almost invariably, Hilbig's figures lead a double life. They must hide themselves from others, and often *from* themselves. Usually they are manual laborers, who write in the evening. Their words and deeds, determined by this permanent need for secrecy, awaken suspicion both on the part of the other literary figures and on the part of the reader, who is continually led to presume some degree of falsehood or self-deception in their statements.

The real world is difficult to discern in Hilbig's narrative realm. Hilbig's narrations are structured around fluid transitions between dream and actuality, between delusion and reality, and between experiences and uncertain memories of those experiences. The narrative scenery is often portrayed in terms of diffuse light, mist, smoke, "Dusk and shadow," "Half-dark," "Twilight," "Darkness." His figures are often at home in these dusky regions: they do not take on clear physical contours—indeed, they avoid light. The instability in the personalities of Hilbig's figures is reflected in their spatial placement: they perceive "no 'ground under their feet,' [they] lack any solid underground, and live, with regard to their sensations, in a 'mire'."[7] In fact, his figures display a proclivity for subterranean regions: they prefer to lurk in cellars and catacombs. They explore quite literally the underside of civilization: the foundations of the city and the mineshafts that bore through the rural landscape of East Germany. In addition to being unable to find a hold in their environment spatially, Hilbig's figures are temporally disoriented: they are never on time, and they perceive time itself as having come to a standstill.

If Hilbig's work figuratively renders the world a realm of uncertainty, this rendering is self-reflexive: Hilbig's prose centers of the unreliability of storytelling (*erzählen*) and language in general:

> the nouns, which I [the fictional author that narrates an account of his own writing processes] had at my disposal to this end [of storytelling], showed themselves again and again as deceptive means, and they cea-selessly held the powerlessness of all descriptions before my eyes [...] they appeared, with regard to the nuances of the visible, to be at most poor bits of *information*.[8]

Hilbig portrays creative writers in such a way that one inevitably sees his portrayal as a representation of his own writing activity: "there was a series of extinguished nouns, I [again Hilbig's fictional author] attempted to bring them to life with attributes, tried to imbue their gaunt meagerness with color, but now I saw a parade of masks, the faces of made-up corpses."[9]

Hilbig's worker–writers are perpetually unsatisfied with what they write. Wittstock places Hilbig's work in the literary tradition of a radical skepti-cism of language exemplified by Hugo von Hoffmannsthal, Ingeborg Bachmann, and Thomas Bernhard.

It is not Hilbig's intention, however, to develop a clandestine, non-metaphorical language, on Wittstock's view. Rather, Hilbig's antirealism is understood as an emphatic form of realism, to the extent that the literary representation of the *insufficiency* of language to represent the world is con-sidered the nearest possible approximation to a realistic representation of the world.[10] But it is not just language's insufficiency in representing the world that Hilbig doubts, but also the phenomenal world in general. Hilbig portrays that which is visible as a deceptive surface. Whereas one cannot directly represent what lies behind this surface through language, on Hilbig's view, the *fact* that the visible is only a surface *can* be depicted. Hilbig's attempt to render what is visible *as* an illusive surface is furthermore understood as a historical perspective, Wittstock argues, a stereoscopical reading of the past on the basis of the apparent world in the present. Hilbig is fundamentally concerned with representing that which is visible as the sedimentation of history, and herein he takes a political turn. Hilbig portrays life as coming into being out of the ashes, out of the refuse of earlier generations, and the earlier generations with which he is concerned are particularly German:

> Oh, stumbling over mass graves [...] oh, in a land composed of tracts of mass graves, comparable to a honeycomb of mass graves, land covering the mass graves with philosophies, risen above the mass graves from the ruins, above the mass graves of the dictatorship of the proletariat.[11]

Hilbig's portrayal aims at exposing the unsightly underside of contemporary Germany by drawing a connection between the fascist and communist dictatorships of its collective past.

Wittstock argues that a common structural element in Hilbig's narrative texts is to be found in the principle of excommunication.[12] In its original psychoanalytic usage, the term *excommunication* refers to those regions of the human psyche that, due to social constraints, must be repressed and excluded from communication in order to give clearer contours to one's identity. These repressed forces do not lose their sway over individuals, however, and are ultimately expressed through neuroses and other psychic illnesses. Wittstock notes that Hilbig thematizes various such repressions in his texts: sexuality (in *Die Weiber*), death (*Alte Abdeckerei*), and nature (*Die Kunde von den Bäumen*).[13] The principle of excommunication is emblematized in Hilbig's protagonists, who, invariably, are social outsiders that pursue the objects of their own neurotic obsessions in an unrestrained manner. The principle of excommunication, which excludes by its nature, is a dialectical principle, however, and ultimately serves, Wittstock argues, inclusion and the clear definition of a norm.[14]

Wittstock's notion of excommunication is in fact useful in the context of *"I,"* in which this dialectic of the trangression and the definition of norms is a central topic, and I turn now to my own brief look at the novel. Here the infraction and consolidation of a norm concerns the relation between underground literature and the East German *Staatssicherheitsdienst* (Stasi). Hilbig's novel aims at an illustration of their codependence: the Stasi needs, in the end, to support a resistant underground in order to justify its own existence and to help the state it serves to take on clearer contours, in keeping with the byword "power needs an enemy"; and the literary scene requires the Stasi as the object of its moral derision in order to endow its own aesthetic endeavor with purpose and themselves, its members, with a distinct identity. On first appearance such a construction seems purely fictive, but the public treatment of various East German authors implicated as unofficial informants for the Stasi seem to bear out at least one side of this codependence. The poet Sascha Anderson is one such case: the revelation that Anderson, previously considered a headman of the underground literary avant-garde in Berlin's Prenzlauer Berg, had cooperated with the Stasi moved other literary personalities to denounce his work and deny it any *aesthetic* quality whatsoever.

Hilbig's *"I"* centers on a figure that has a great deal in common with the real-life Anderson. In *"I,"* Hilbig has to some degree moved away from the surreal landscapes of his earlier works to an ironic realism, centering more or less on one, however schizophrenic, figure. The antihero of the novel is M.W., who works under the covername of "Cambert," as an unofficial informant of the Stasi. His *operativer Vorgang* (Stasi-talk for the person he is ordered to observe) is known as "Reader." "Reader" is a caricature of the Prenzlauer Berg literary figure, a radically avant-garde author who dabbles in French poststructuralism and welcomes the admiration of the "Szene" (scene) that attends public recitals of his incomprehensible texts. "Cambert" takes precise notes on the readings, observes the audience, and torments himself with his meticulous reports on the audience members to the Stasi.

At the same time, "Cambert" is a struggling lyrical writer himself. Indeed, for M.W., alias "Cambert," literary writing and the writing of Stasi reports become indistinguishable components of his activity. The novel takes place in the last years of the GDR and manifests an end-time atmosphere in the dubious "I" that makes up the title: the novel is initially told from the perspective of the agent M.W., but this perspective slips into the third person and subsequently switches between that of Cambert and M.W. One quickly loses a sense of who (or which aspect of whom) is speaking, as the apostrophized "I" of the title becomes a marker of empty signification. Both temporally and spatially there is no less confusion: M.W. often slips into his underground hideout in the cellars under East Berlin, where he has set up a comfortable red chair next to the external wall of the Stasi headquarters in the Normannenstraße. It is not clear where what is narrated when: has he fallen asleep in the S-Bahn only to wake up 200 pages later, or was he in fact dreaming in his red chair the entire time? M.W. himself has lost his sense of time and abilities of self-orientation: he has sold his soul to the Stasi, the anonymous, timeless, and ubiquitous, documenting entity.

M.W.'s only intellectual contact is his immediate superior in the Stasi, codename "Feuerbach," who lives up to his namesake by incessantly philosophizing, and who expounds on the intimate relation between underground literature and state security, because without the Stasi, so goes his argument, the literary scene would have no reason to exist. Hilbig's novel thematizes a ubiquitous *simulation:* the GDR appears as a moral vacuum, in which accountability is fully lost in fictional representations, both those of the Stasi reports and those of literature. The commonality and even complicity between state security and literature consists in their creation of absolute fictions. And their secret identity is exhibited in the split personality of M.W./Cambert.

In the overwhelmingly positive critical response to Hilbig's novel, the central mode of validating the work aesthetically is the attribution of *authenticity* in various forms. First, purely in his *presence as an author* Hilbig is characterized as genuine: "original,"[15] "the poet as an ingenious naif,"[16] "the Hölderlin from Saxony."[17] His novel is held to be genuine by virtue of its self-reflexivity and self-criticality: "'*I*' is a novel [...] about the temptations of the writer, his voyeurism, interpretive fury";[18] Hilbig's writing is "authentic and [it] truly oversteps boundaries, dissolving barriers to thought."[19]

Second, his fiction represents *autobiographical truth:* the split between "I and He" in the novel reflect Hilbig's own experience as a writer and laborer:

> These doublings and splittings of the I correspond to Hilbig's authentic experience as a laborer in the GDR [...]. In his role as writer, [...] the

speechless existence of the laborer turns into language. This language is a singular, disoriented searching movement. It corresponds to a subjectivity that cannot conceive itself, [and] the language comes into being out of a constant, reciprocal repulsion between the laborer's and the writer's forms of existence.[20]

Third, Hilbig's novel is considered authentic to the extent that it captures the *specificity of a particular socio-historical situation:* Hilbig's "Ich" is heeded "[a] social novel about the end time of the GDR,"[21] alternately, "a grand metaphor for the GDR."[22] The end of the GDR is emblematized in the writer-spy figure of "Cambert" and the loss of language that he undergoes: "a language that fixes how one loses his language."[23] The fictive loss of language here symbolizes the factual disorientation of the last moments of the GDR state and its subsequent new status as an extension of the FRG. Helmut Böttiger praises Hilbig's marriage of aesthetic appeal and historical relevance: "a fantastic, linguistically powerful novel which connects immediate contemporary history and literary vision in a tremendous manner."[24] One final sample of this kind of appraisal: "There has been no other book to date, that could make the attitude towards life in the GDR more vivid and also more understandable. [...] At many points images arise that tell the entire history of this country."[25]

Where the critique becomes interesting for my argument is where it separates the aesthetic success of Hilbig's novel from its political content: "And *although* this first novel about the entanglements between literature and Stasi is, by virtue of its content, a political phenomenon: the undertaking is resolved in a literarily persuasive way."[26] The undercurrent of this kind of appraisal is that the aesthetic evaluation of literature need not consider, or indeed can be carried out *despite* the normative content of the work at hand. Here is where aesthetic criticism is self-contradictory: in the insistence of the independence of aesthetic validity from nonaesthetic forms of validity. The argument that the complex relation between literature and state security is rendered in a way that is *aesthetically* convincing implies that the historical situation of the last years of the GDR, although fictively portrayed, is *accurately* and *appropriately* rendered.

And Hilbig's own description of his activity as a writer, in interviews, for instance, also reveals the trend of self-inconsistency seen in criticism. Hilbig asserts: "The task of the writer is not to offer proposals as Brecht said [...] The only thing that I want through writing is *to express myself.* That is more than one might think. Literature is more something animalistic than something intellectual. Something libidinal. At any rate, not a task of convincing."[27] Here Hilbig sees literary rationality purely as *expressive rationality.* Another citation: "[Literature] does not imitate reality, rather what is creative. [...] If it succeeds at that it has accomplished something. No other medium can do that."[28] Indeed, Hilbig makes the notion of the independence of expressive rationality from truth and rightness claims explicit: "If an analysis [of social mechanisms] has arisen within [my] texts, then it was surely not my intention."[29] Ironically, Hilbig's claim about his intentions only to faithfully express his personal experiences itself reveals a disingenuousness: the publication of a novel is an act that is performed under the presupposition that what is written can resonate in an audience. Particularly in the case of an author that portrays, albeit in the form of one figure, the problematic imbrications of two institutions with far-reaching influence in the GDR, he cannot justly claim to be attempting to represent only his own experience.

How is such a claim to be reconciled, for instance, with Hilbig's self-understanding as a writer, apparent in the following citation? "Besides, I write against forgetting [the ways of life in the GDR]. Today already, one forgets what the streets, which have suddenly become pedestrian zones, looked like. Whether one loved them or hated them, they were authentic and smelled. That definitely does have something to do with loss."[30]

The portrayal of authenticity that Hilbig envisions, I argue, necessarily, operates under normative presuppositions. These only become explicit in talks of Hilbig's, such as his "Kamenzer Talk," where, in his disillusionment with the process and consequences of German unification, he characterizes Western mentalities as "colonialism." Another citation: "Perhaps it would be prudent to consider the act of reunification to be a kind of sodomy with dependents."[31]

The inconsistency evident in Hilbig's own reflections on his authorship that is interesting for the purposes of my argument here is the following: the *disingenuousness* of reducing one's own writing activity to *expressivity*. This is the traditional withdrawal of the artist into an autonomous realm of aesthetic validity that is allegedly exempt from critique along other dimensions of validity and of the reduction of aesthetic validity to expressive validity. This reduction of aesthetic validity to expressive genuineness is, as seen above, also present in some, albeit positive, criticism of Hilbig's *"I."* It is not the case that one can evaluate a particular text politically and, fully separate from that, on the basis of purely aesthetic standards. Rather the validation (or rejection) of a work *on aesthetic grounds* already contains an endorsement or contestation of its claims of normative and descriptive validity. That is, one cannot hold that a text is aesthetically successful or not without simultaneously raising claims about its truth- and normative content. This is part of the point behind holding aesthetic validity to contain subsidiary claims of the three forms of validity that Habermas explicates.

That the claim of aesthetic validity contains normative and descriptive aspects does not alone make aesthetic validity a form of *interference*, however. The interference, in literary rationality, arises through *prima facie* conflicts in the equally valid claims that are made by, and with regard to, a piece of literature. The fact that Hilbig was not himself a Stasi conspirator, for instance, does not nullify the argument that his character's biography reflects his own biography. Both can be true. Hilbig's construction of the doubled figure of Stasi man and writer is carried out as a counterfactual speculation on the intimate relation between the perpetrator and the victim in the Stasi surveillance system. This is underlain, in turn, by a normative claim. Putting both aspects, victim and perpetrator, into one figure brings a perhaps uncomfortable perspective on the question of accountability for the negative consequences of the security activities of the GDR state. By aligning alleged resistance with cooperation, Hilbig complicates the moral question behind the Stasi debate. Hilbig does not add fuel to the fire of the scandal-hungry German public by relying on a clearly defined scapegoat in the shape of the Stasi but rather challenges his audience to reflect on her/his own role in the machinery of oppression.

This critique is not limited to societal conditions in the former GDR, however. The ubiquitous simulation portrayed in Hilbig's novel refers just as well to the media society of West Germany as it does to the Stasi apparatus. The "I" of M.W./Cambert is an empty citation in the same way that the prepackaged identities of media society, in billboards and television advertisements, for instance, promise but fail to endow an authentic identity. Although he tends toward it in his explicitly political speeches, Hilbig is not evoking an authenticity with regard to the former East, the so-called "Ostalgie." But his psychopathology of East German society also does not turn for commiseration to the West. Authentic is the portrayal of society that radically questions the varied semblances of authenticity in that society: this would serve as a paraphrase of Hilbig's aesthetic program. The authenticity claim in Hilbig's novel refers to the shared experience both in the Stasi-supported state and in contemporary media society of a lack of authenticity.

Hilbig's "*I*" is centrally concerned with the allegorical representation of a particular sociohistorical situation. What is evident from this brief look at the text is how the narrator's concatenation of pronouns, specifically the alternation between the *we* and *I* perspectives, renders this allegory one of a shareable complex of experience. The relative openness in meaning, i.e. the relative nonspecificity of subjective experience despite the autobiographical details and historical references that are present throughout the narrative, is a product of the indistinctness of the distinction between personal memory and shared history. Hilbig's subterranean cellar world and his narrator's topographical surveys of the metropolis of Berlin are the sites where this link between individual and collective memory is established.

In this interconnection, and through the portrayal of an inauthentic subjective identity, of the specter of his own apostrophized "*I*" that haunts the protagonist, the narration ultimately generates a claim to an intersubjective authenticity. This is one and the same as a claim of the shareability of the representation of the historical situation that the text embodies, and is taken as the primary criterion for measuring the communicative potential and aesthetic quality of Hilbig's "*I*." The text understands itself (and its critics evaluate it aesthetically with an eye to its success in doing so) as throwing the relation between personal identity and shared history in the former GDR and newly unified Germany into a radically new light. The kind of rationality operating here is the literary rationality I made a case for above. The end of this literary rationality is not merely subjective expression but the negotiation of historically relevant complexes of shareable experience. To the extent that Hilbig's *"I"* and its published reception are fundamentally concerned with the features of shareability and historical relevance, they not only illustrate the theoretical account of literary rationality given above but are also emblematic of what is at issue in the literature on German unification and its reception.

5 Concluding Remark

This study began by identifying an inconsistency in Habermas's account of the societal role of literature, an inconsistency that it sets out to resolve. On the one hand Habermas recognizes the valuable contribution made by literature to the cultural and political public spheres, I argued. This recognition can be read out of his recent political essays and his exchange with and remarks on literary figures, particularly around the time of the German–German literary controversy of 1990. On the other hand, I argue, Habermas's theoretical work effectively restricts literary rationality to the realm of autonomous art and a concern for the truthfulness of subjective self-expression. In this regard, I have argued that Habermas's account of literary rationality is a reductive account that leaves the communicative potential of literature underdeveloped. In consideration of his more positive appraisal of the contribution of the literary public sphere to the public sphere at large, I suggested that the historical and literary context of post-unification Germany provides a backdrop against which elements of Habermas's more political, less theoretical publications can help improve his own theoretical account of aesthetic rationality.

A novel such as Hilbig's "*I*" and its published reception show in particular how the literary institution performs the peculiar kind of "needs interpretation" that Habermas envisions for aesthetic practice: Hilbig's portrayal of the lack of authenticity in the (pre-unification) German Democratic Republic (GDR) from the perspective of a post-unification Germany in which authentic personal and collective identities are also, although differently, stifled, is the portrayal of precisely one of the "normative deficits" of unification that Habermas criticizes. In looking briefly at Hilbig's novel, it was not so much my goal to evaluate the novel aesthetically myself, as to show what is at stake in aesthetic evaluations of the novel: both the validity claims that critiques of the novel raise with regard to the novel and what about the novel redeems those claims. I wanted to demonstrate that to whatever extent critiques of the novel might refer to the latter's aesthetic "well-formedness," the criteria of subjective truthfulness, normative rightness, and descriptive truth all play a role in validating or invalidating the novel, and that these criteria play this role precisely to the extent that they support or reject a claim of authenticity, i.e. a claim to portray a shareable experience, paradigmatic for a particular sociohistorical context. To the extent that Hilbig's novel, in the performative stance it takes up with regard to its audience, challenges its audiences views on the objective, social, and their respective subjective worlds and on the relations between these, it has a communicative function. Whether or not a particular reader accepts the authenticity claim of Hilbig's novel, is not, as *TCA* argues, the same as whether the reader attributes truthfulness to the author's self-representation through the novel (see 3.1.2.1).

While it is certainly true that the reader of a text does not approach the reception of a literary text in the same way that she approaches practical problem-solving in the context of everyday situations—in other words, that she does not experience the problems encountered in a novel, for instance, as her own immediate problems—there is a sense in which the aesthetically valid text articulates an experience that she can reasonably imagine to be her own and furthermore enables the finding of a changed practical relation to the world in light of this relayed, shareable experience. For this reason, it is not enough to hold that aesthetic validity lies in mere world-disclosure, as Habermas does. And for this same reason I have tried to argue here that the operation of aesthetic rationality does not merely put forth ways of *looking* at the world, and that an artwork is not aesthetically valid merely on the basis of its successful *reorientation* of its recipients, but rather that the operation of aesthetic rationality also, through its reorienting effects, gives rise to ways of *acting* in the world. For these reasons this study gave an account of the literary institution as a forum for communicative reason, and the literary public sphere as a unique contributor to the political public sphere.

Notes

1 INTRODUCTION

1 Jürgen Habermas, *Strukturwandel der Öffentlichkeit: Untersuchungen zu einer Kategorie der bürgerlichen Gesellschaft,* 5th edn, with a new foreword (Frankfurt: Suhrkamp, 1990). Hereafter referred to as *STPS.*

2 See Peter Uwe Hohendahl, *Literarische Kultur im Zeitalter des Liberalismus 1830–1870* (Munich: C.H. Beck, 1985).

3 In Habermas, *Theory of Communicative Action* (Boston, Mass.: Beacon Press, 1987), p. 328, endnote 22, Habermas cites Leo Löwenthal, *Das bürgerliche Bewußtsein in der Literatur,* Gesammelte Schriften, vol. II (Frankfurt: Suhrkamp, 1981). The Habermas title is hereafter referred to as *TCA.*

4 Habermas, "Was ist ein Volk? Zum politischen Selbstverständnis der Geisteswissenschaften im Vormärz, am Beispiel der Frankfurter Germanistenversammlung von 1846," *Die postnationale Konstellation: politische Essays* (Frankfurt: Suhrkamp, 1998), pp. 13–36.

5 In Christa Wolf, *Auf dem Weg nach Tabou: Texte 1990–1994* (Munich: Luchterhand, 1995), pp. 140–155. Habermas's letter is reprinted in Habermas, *Die Normalität einer Berliner Republik: politische Schriften VIII* (Frankfurt: Suhrkamp, 1995), pp. 101–111.

6 The German–German literary controversy (*Literaturstreit*) arose in the context of the publication of Christa Wolf's *What Remains* (*Was bleibt*), an autobiographical reconstruction of a day in the life of a writer who is observed by the East German State Security Service (the Stasi). Critics, most importantly among them Frank Schirrmacher of the *Frankfurter Allgemeine Zeitung,* Ulrich Greiner of *Die Zeit,* and Karl-Heinz Bohrer of *Merkur,* gave the book devastating reviews and took the occasion to broadly denounce the aesthetics of conviction (*Gesinnungsästhetik*) that it allegedly presented. Schirrmacher, for instance, saw the "aesthetics of conviction" to be a weakness common to most of postwar German literature, both East and West. The aesthetics free of moralizing and politicizing elements that they envisioned for a new German literature was itself, however, clearly bound up, especially in Bohrer, with its own political claims about the proper historical self-understanding of postwar Germany and a new, positive post-Wall sense of German national identity.

7 See in particular, Habermas, *Die nachholende Revolution: politische Schriften VII* (Frankfurt: Suhrkamp, 1990); *Die Vergangenheit als Zukunft* (Munich: Piper, 1993); and *Die Normalität einer Berliner Republik: politische Schriften VIII* (Frankfurt: Suhrkamp, 1995).

8 Habermas, "Nochmals: Zur Identität der Deutschen: Ein einig Volk von aufgebrachten Wirtschaftsbürgern?" *Die nachholende Revolution,* p. 217. Translation is mine.

2 THE THEORY OF COMMUNICATIVE ACTION: A SYNOPSIS

1 Habermas, *Theory of Communicative Action* (Boston, Mass.: Beacon Press, 1987), vol. I, p. 20. Hereafter referred to as *TCA*.
2 *TCA*, vol. I, p. 20.
3 See *TCA*, vol. I, pp. 20–21.
4 See *TCA*, vol. I, p. 26.
5 See *TCA*, vol. I, p. 37–38.
6 *TCA*, vol. I, p. 39.
7 *TCA*, vol. I, p. 41.
8 *TCA*, vol. I, p. 42.
9 See *TCA*, vol. I, pp. 41–42.
10 *TCA*, vol. I, p. 86.
11 See *TCA*, vol. I, p. 86.
12 See *TCA*, vol. I, p. 86.
13 *TCA*, vol. I, p. 95.
14 See *TCA*, vol. I, p. 101.
15 See *TCA*, vol. I, pp. 163–164.
16 *TCA*, vol. I, p. 177.
17 *TCA*, vol. I, p. 183.
18 See *TCA*, vol. I, p. 237, Fig. 10.
19 See *TCA*, vol. I, p. 236.
20 *TCA*, vol. I, p. 238.
21 See *TCA*, vol. I, p. 239–240.
22 *TCA*, vol. I, p. 240.
23 *TCA*, vol. I, p. 275.
24 *TCA*, vol. I, p. 277.
25 Habermas, "Exkurs zur Einebnung des Gattungsunterschiedes zwichen Philosophie und Literatur," *Der philosophische Diskurs der Moderne* (Frankfurt: Suhrkamp, 1985), pp. 219–247. Translation is mine.
26 See *TCA*, vol. I, pp. 285–287.
27 See *TCA*, vol. I, pp. 288–289.
28 See *TCA*, vol. I, p. 289.
29 *TCA*, vol. I, p. 293.
30 *TCA*, vol. I, p. 293.
31 *TCA*, vol. I, p. 294.
32 *TCA*, vol. I, p. 295.
33 See *TCA*, vol. I, p. 296.
34 See *TCA*, vol. I, p. 297.
35 *TCA*, vol. I, p. 302.
36 *TCA*, vol. I, p. 303.
37 *TCA*, vol. I, p. 303.
38 *TCA*, vol. I, p. 303.
39 See *TCA*, vol. II, pp. 328–329.
40 *TCA*, vol. II, p. 329.
41 *TCA*, vol. II, p. 330.
42 See *TCA*, vol. II, p. 330.
43 *TCA*, vol. II, p. 389.
44 *TCA*, vol. II, p. 390.
45 See *TCA*, vol. II, pp. 397–398.
46 *TCA*, vol. II, p. 398.
47 See *TCA*, vol. II, p. 398.
48 *TCA*, vol. II, p. 398.

3 LITERARY RATIONALITY AND COMMUNICATIVE REASON

1 Habermas, *Theory of Communicative Action* (Boston, Mass.: Beacon Press, 1987), vol. I, p. 305. Hereafter referred to as *TCA*.
2 See *TCA*, vol. I, p. 331.
3 *TCA*, vol. I, p. 331.
4 See *TCA*, vol. I, p. 331.
5 *TCA*, vol. I, p. 295.
6 Martin Seel gives this definition of the attribute *performative* in "Kunst, Wahrheit und Welterschließung [Art, Truth and World-Disclosure]," in Franz Koppe (ed.), *Perspektiven der Kunstphilosophie: Texte und Diskussionen* (Frankfurt: Suhrkamp, 1991), p. 57, footnote 23. Hereafter referred to as "ATWD." Translation is mine.
7 *TCA*, vol. I, p. 20.
8 See *TCA*, vol. I, p. 20.
9 See Seel, "ATWD," esp. pp. 42–43.
10 See *TCA*, vol. I, pp. 38ff.
11 See *TCA*, vol. I, p. 42.
12 It is an altogether different question whether Habermas can get around this seeming inconsistency by maintaining the *universality of the truthfulness claim* while pointing out the *specificity of the cultural value standards* legitimized by the truthfulness claim (in art criticism, for instance).
13 *TCA*, vol. I, p. 177.
14 *TCA*, vol. I, pp. 177–178.
15 *TCA*, vol. I, p. 183.
16 See *TCA*, vol. I, pp. 236–237.
17 Habermas apparently intends a broad notion of *erotic practice*, which refers to all the varied forms of self-oriented engagement with one's desires and perceived needs.
18 See *TCA*, vol. I, pp. 239–240.
19 *TCA*, vol. I, p. 238.
20 See *TCA*, vol. I, p. 239.
21 *TCA*, vol. I, pp. 238–239.
22 *TCA*, vol. I, p. 240.
23 Habermas stresses that whereas communication-oriented uses of language also aim at success, one can determine on the basis of the intuitive knowledge of the discourse participants which orientation is decisive.
24 See *TCA*, vol. I, p. 91.
25 *TCA*, vol. I, p. 95.
26 See *TCA*, vol. I, pp. 306–307.
27 *TCA*, vol. I, pp. 306–307.
28 *TCA*, vol. I, p. 331.
29 Habermas's demonstration that (certain) *perlocutionary* aims are (fully) realized *only if one conceals them* is convincing. If I tell someone, "I want to intimidate you by demonstrating my superior knowledge of Hegelian philosophy" I will obviously not have the same effect on him/her as when I simply attempt to demonstrate this allegedly superior knowledge. Habermas's claim that *illocutionary* goals are only successful *if pronounced* is not convincing, however. I can obligate myself to certain actions or the demonstration of facts or justification of normative presuppositions without explicitly referring to those obligations. This is in fact a logical consequence of Habermas's point that contestable validity claims must be raised *at least implicitly* in order for a speech act to belong to communicative action.
30 Jürgen Habermas, "Handlungen, Sprechakte, sprachlich vermittelte Interaktionen und Lebenswelt [Actions, Speech-Acts, Linguistically Mediated

Interactions and Lifeworld]," in *Nachmetaphysisches Denken* (Frankfurt: Suhrkamp, 1988), pp. 63–104. Hereafter referred to as "ASIL." Translation is mine.

31 Habermas, "ASIL," p. 79.

32 Jürgen Habermas, "Ein anderer Ausweg aus der Subjektphilosophie: kommunikative vs. subjektzentrierte Vernunft," in *Der philosophische Diskurs der Moderne* (Frankfurt: Suhrkamp, 1985), p. 366. Hereafter referred to as "Ausweg." Translation is mine.

33 Seel, "ATWD," p. 52.

34 This reduction stands, just as it had in *TCA*, next to the other two complexes of "moral-practical" and "cognitive-instrumental" rationality.

35 See Habermas, "Exkurs zur Einebnung des Gattungsunterschiedes zwichen Philosophie und Literatur," *Der philosophische Diskurs der Moderne* (Frankfurt: Suhrkamp, 1985), pp. 219–247. Hereafter referred to as "Exkurs."

36 Habermas, "Exkurs," p. 236.

37 Richard Ohmann, "Speech-Acts and the Definition of Literature," *Philosophy and Rhetoric*, 4 (1971): 17. Cited in "Exkurs," p. 236.

38 Ohmann, "Speech-Acts and the Definition of Literature," p. 17. Cited in Habermas, "Exkurs," p. 236.

39 Habermas, "Exkurs," p. 236.

40 Habermas, "Exkurs," p. 243.

41 Jürgen Habermas, "Philosophie und Wissenschaft als Literatur? [Philosophy and Science as Literature?]," in *Nachmetaphysisches Denken* (Frankfurt: Suhrkamp, 1988), pp. 242–263. Hereafter referred to as "PSL." Translation is mine.

42 Habermas, "PSL," p. 261.

43 Habermas, "PSL," p. 262.

44 See Habermas, "PSL," p. 292.

45 Theodor W. Adorno, *Ästhetische Theorie*, Gesammelte Schriften, Vol. VII (Frankfurt: Suhrkamp, 1997). Hereafter referred to as *AT*. Translation is mine.

46 Franz Koppe, *Grundbegriffe der Ästhetik* (Frankfurt: Suhrkamp, 1983). Hereafter referred to as *FCA*. Translation is mine.

47 Koppe, *FCA*, p. 88. Here Koppe relies on an argument originally made by Herbert Marcuse in "Über den affirmativen Charakter der Kultur," in *Kultur und Gesellschaft I* (Frankfurt: Suhrkamp, 1965), pp. 56–101. Marcuse there points out the fundamental absurdity involved in theorizing art when one posits competing kinds of truth for art and theory.

48 Koppe, *FCA*, p. 112.

49 See Koppe, *FCA*, pp. 122–123.

50 *Innovation*, in the sense of enabling new perception through new distinctions and new systems of differentiation, is the primary business of the sciences, for example; the reflexive focus on the *process* of production without an eye to utility is also characteristic of craftmaking, for instance; *indeterminacy* and *ambiguity* are also exemplified in political and legal texts, for example, where the interpretive freedom of the text's recipient is presupposed and generally intended by its authors; *fictionality* is also a defining trait of hypotheses and mathematical problems, for instance; and *exemplarity*, the demonstration of the general through the particular, is characteristic of every naming of an example.

51 Koppe, *FCA*, p. 125.

52 Koppe, *FCA*, p. 134.

53 Koppe is careful to distinguish *connotative* from *associative* here. Whereas *associative* designates those ideas and feelings that accompany an *individual's* reception, *connotative* designates *intersubjectively* recognized, implied meanings (see Koppe, *FCA*, pp. 128–129). Koppe cites Kant as the first to have identified the connotative character of art, when the latter writes of the "'multiplicity of partial representations of an 'aesthetic idea' [...], 'for which no expression

designates a definite concept could be found' and which, nonetheless would make 'the unnameable in the emotional state' [...] 'generally communicable'." Immanuel Kant, *Kritik der Urteilskraft,* ed. Otfried Hoffe, Edition B §49, 197, according to original pagination (Berlin: Akademie Verlag, 2008) cited from Koppe, *FCA,* pp. 133–134. Hereafter referred to as *CJ.* Translation is mine.

54 Koppe, *FCA,* p. 135.
55 Jürgen Habermas, "Bewußtmachende oder rettende Kritik–die Aktualität Walter Benjamins," in *Kultur und Kritk* (Frankfurt: Suhrkamp, 1973), p. 33. Translation is mine.
56 Jürgen Habermas, "Zwei Bemerkungen zum praktischen Diskurs. Paul Lorenzen zum 60. Geburtstag," in *Zur Rekonstruktion des historischen Materialismus* (Frankfurt: Suhrkamp, 1976), p. 334. Translation is mine.
57 See Koppe, *FCA,* p. 142.
58 Koppe, *FCA,* p. 136.
59 Koppe, *FCA,* p. 136.
60 Koppe, *FCA,* p. 221, endnote 22.
61 Koppe, *FCA,* p. 152.
62 Koppe, *FCA,* p. 155.
63 Koppe, *FCA,* p. 134; my emphasis.
64 Albrecht Wellmer, "Wahrheit, Schein, Versöhnung: Adornos ästhetische Rettung der Moderne," in Jürgen Habermas and Ludwig von Friedeburg (eds), *Adorno-Konferenz 1983* (Frankfurt: Suhrkamp, 1983), pp. 138–178. Reprinted in *Zur Dialektik von Moderne und Postmoderne: Vernunftkritik nach Adorno* (Frankfurt: Suhrkamp, 1985), pp. 9–47. I cite the latter edition, and the translations are mine.
65 Theodor Adorno and Max Horkheimer, *Dialektik der Aufklärung,* in Theodor Adorno, *Gesammelte Schriften,* Vol. III (Frankfurt: Suhrkamp, 1997). Hereafter referred to as *DoE.*
66 Wellmer, *Dialectic,* p. 10.
67 Wellmer, *Dialectic,* p. 12.
68 Adorno, *Negative Dialektik,* Gesammelte Schriften, Vol. VI (Frankfurt: Suhrkamp, 1997), p. 27. Translation is mine.
69 Wellmer, *Dialectic,* p. 12.
70 Wellmer, *Dialectic,* p. 12.
71 Wellmer, *Dialectic,* p. 13.
72 See *AT,* p. 185.
73 *AT,* p. 193.
74 Adorno, "Fragment über Musik und Sprache," *Musikalische Schriften I–III,* Gesammelte Schriften, Vol. XVI (Frankfurt: Suhrkamp, 1997), p. 252. Translation is mine.
75 Wellmer, *Dialectic,* p. 15.
76 See Wellmer, *Dialectic,* p. 15.
77 Wellmer, *Dialectic,* p. 16.
78 Wellmer, *Dialectic,* p. 20.
79 Wellmer, *Dialectic,* p. 19.
80 See Habermas, *TCA,* vol. I, p. 523.
81 See Wellmer, *Dialectic,* p. 29.
82 Wellmer, *Dialectic,* p. 29. Hans Robert Jauss, *Ästhetische Erfahrung und literarische Hermeneutik* (Frankfurt: Suhrkamp, 1982). Cited from Wellmer, *FCA,* p. 29. Translation is mine.
83 Wellmer, *Dialectic,* p. 31; my emphasis.
84 Wellmer, *Dialectic,* p. 31.
85 See Wellmer, *Dialectic,* p. 32.
86 Wellmer, *Dialectic,* p. 32.

87 Wellmer, *Dialectic*, p. 35.
88 Wellmer, *Dialectic*, p. 36.
89 Wellmer, *Dialectic*, p. 37.
90 Wellmer, *Dialectic*, p. 43.
91 Wellmer, *Dialectic*, p. 43.
92 Martin Seel, *Die Kunst der Entzweiung: zum Begriff der ästhetischen Rationalität* (Frankfurt: Suhrkamp, 1985). Hereafter referred to as *AD*. Translation is mine.
93 Seel, *AD*, p. 17.
94 Seel, *AD*, p. 29.
95 Seel, *AD*, p. 30.
96 Seel, *AD*, p. 31.
97 Seel, *AD*, pp. 37–38.
98 Kant, *CJ*, §60.
99 Kant, *CJ*, §1.
100 Seel, *AD*, p. 45.
101 Karl-Heinz Bohrer, *Plötzlichkeit: zum Augenblick des ästhetischen Scheins* (Frankfurt: Suhrkamp, 1981). Translation is mine. Hereafter referred to as *Suddenness*.
102 Bohrer, *Suddenness*, p. 105.
103 See Bohrer, *Suddenness*, pp. 40, 78, 103, 132.
104 Bohrer, *Suddenness*, p. 125.
105 Bohrer, *Suddeness*, p. 13.
106 See Seel, *AD*, pp. 68–69.
107 See Seel, *AD*, p. 69.
108 John Dewey, *Art as Experience* (New York: Capricorn, 1958).
109 For the summary contained in the next two paragraphs I rely heavily on Axel Honneth's review in *Merkur*, 40 (3) (1986): 240–245.
110 In face of the difficulty of accurately rendering the difference in meaning between *eine Erfahrung machen* and *Erfahrung haben* I translate the first of these as "have an experience" and would translate the second of these as "to have experience." The context of usage should make clear which sense is intended, and, in this context, exclusively the first sense is used.
111 Seel, *AD*, pp. 280–281.
112 See Seel, *AD*, p. 281.
113 See Koppe, *FCA*, pp. 147ff., and Habermas, *TCA*, vol. I, p. 20.
114 See Habermas, *TCA*, vol. I, p. 308.
115 See Seel, *AD*, p. 292.
116 Seel, *AD*, p. 292.
117 Seel, *AD*, p. 29.
118 Seel, *AD*, p. 292.
119 Seel indicates that Habermas comes close to making this argument himself, at least as concerns moral argumentation, in *Moralbewußtsein und kommunikatives Handeln* (Frankfurt: Suhrkamp, 1983), p. 115. See also above discussion of Koppe and Habermas on the occasional reliance of moral-practical discourse on (therapeutic critique) and aesthetic practice in 3.2.1.
120 Seel writes: "Ultimately forms of validity are not forms of speech, they are forms of linguistic, language-related and language-mediated action that cannot be reduced to linguistic schemes of this action—to sentence modes and speech act types" ("ATWD," p. 57). Translation is mine.
121 Wellmer, *FCA*, p. 43.
122 Seel, *AD*, p. 329.
123 See Seel, *AD*, p. 330.
124 See original reference in note 6.

125 This does not, per se, imply that truth in art is derived. But coupled with the characterization of truth in art as a phenomenon of interference between the fundamental forms of validity, which Habermas subsequently takes up from Wellmer, this claim yields the thin version of aesthetic validity as a *distinct* form of validity only insofar as it is *not its own* form of validity. On this account, *truth* can hence only be applied metaphorically to art, hence the derived nature of the concept truth in art for Habermas (and Wellmer).

126 See Seel, "ATWD," pp. 42–43.

127 Seel, "ATWD," p. 45.

128 Charles Taylor, "Sprache und Gesellschaft," in Axel Honneth and Hans Joas (eds), *Kommunikatives Handeln: Beiträge zu Jürgen Habermas' Theorie des kommunikativen Handelns* (Frankfurt: Suhrkamp, 1986), pp. 35–52.

129 See Jürgen Habermas, "Questions and Counterquestions," in R. J. Bernstein (ed.), *Habermas and Modernity* (Cambridge, Mass.: MIT Press, 1985); and Habermas, "Ausweg," especially p. 366.

130 Compare Habermas, "Exkurs," pp. 219–247.

131 See Seel, "ATWD," pp. 51–52.

132 Seel, "ATWD," p. 53.

133 Habermas, "Exkurs," p. 243.

134 Habermas, "Exkurs," p. 238.

135 See *Exkurs,* pp. 245–246.

136 Because effectiveness and preferability arguments constitute diagnostic and normative claims, respectively, they cannot establish strong, conceptual necessity. Hence the quotation marks around *necessary.*

137 *Literature* and *literary* are used here in a broad sense to designate all contemporary aesthetic practices in which language is a medium of communication, be it a central or subsidiary role. This includes film and theater.

138 See note 56.

139 Martin Seel, *Die Kunst der Entzweiung: zum Begriff der ästhetischen Rationalität* (Frankfurt: Suhrkamp, 1985) (see above discussion).

4 THE CLAIM OF AUTHENTICITY: WOLFGANG HILBIG AND THE NOVEL *"ICH"*

1 Wolfgang Hilbig, *"Ich"* (*"I"*) (Frankfurt: S. Fischer, 1993). Hereafter referred to as *"I."* Translation is mine. Further, it is important to understand that the title of the book must be *both* italicized and placed in quotation marks. It is italicized for the reason that it is the name of a book. The author also places it in quotation marks to point to the uncertainty of identity of the book's protagonist. The "I" at the level of novel struggles to find his own identity, and finds only transitory or, at best, provisional answers.

2 Uwe Wittstock (ed.), *Wolfgang Hilbig: Materialien zu Leben und Werk* (Frankfurt: S. Fischer, 1994), pp. 229–230. Translation is mine.

3 Wolfgang Hilbig, *Abwesenheit* (Frankfurt: S. Fischer, 1983).

4 Wittstock, *Wolfgang Hilbig,* p. 229.

5 Here Wittstock cites Hilbig's programmatic essay "Über den Tonfall" in his article "Das Prinzip Exkommunikation: Wanderungen in Wolfgang Hilbigs ungeheurer Prosalandschaft," in Uwe Wittstock (ed.), *Wolfgang Hilbig: Materialien zu Leben und Werk* (Frankfurt: S. Fischer, 1994), pp. 229–245.

6 Wittstock, *Wolfgang Hilbig,* p. 230.

7 Wittstock, *Wolfgang Hilbig,* p. 231.

8 Wolfgang Hilbig, *Alte Abdeckerei* (Frankfurt: S. Fischer, 1991), pp. 12–13.

9 Hilbig, *Alte Abdeckerei*, p. 58.

10 See Wittstock, *Wolfgang Hilbig*, p. 234.

11 Hilbig, *Alte Abdeckerei*, pp. 82–83.

12 Wittstock, *Wolfgang Hilbig*, p. 238.

13 See Wittstock, *Wolfgang Hilbig*, especially p. 238.

14 See Wittstock, *Wolfgang Hilbig*, especially p. 238.

15 Helmut Böttiger, "Dichtung als Geheimdienst," *Frankfurter Rundschau*, 30, February 5, 1994, pp. ZB 2.

16 Hans Peter Kunisch, "Lust an der Freiheit, die ich meine," *Süddeutsche Zeitung*, 64, March 18, 1998, p. 20.

17 Karl Corino, "Hölderlin aus Sachsen," *Stuttgarter Zeitung*, 292, December 19, 1983, p. 11.

18 Tobias Gohlis, "Das Leben–ein Traum der Staatssicherheit," *Stuttgarter Zeitung*, 230, October 5, 1993, p. 1.

19 Gohlis, "Das Leben–ein Traum der Staatssicherheit."

20 Böttiger, "Dichtung als Geheimdienst," p. ZB 2.

21 Dorothea von Törne, "Wie eine Ratte im Labyrinth," *Neue Zeit*, 4, September 4, 1993, p. 14.

22 Helmut Böttiger, "Ein großer Naiver," *Frankfurter Rundschau*, 90, April 18, 1997, p. 9.

23 Lutz Rathenow, "In den Kellern," *Die Welt*, October 5, 1993, p. 4.

24 Helmut Böttiger, "Der Schatten der Existenz, der Genitiv des Menschen," *Frankfurter Rundschau*, August 14, 1993, p. ZB 4.

25 Frank Schirrmacher, "Wir waren der Schatten des Lebens, wir waren der Tod," *Frankfurter Allgemeine Zeitung*, 231, October 5, 1993, p. L1.

26 Cornelia Geißler, "Cambert, der Spitzel stinkt," *Berliner Zeitung*, 234, October 6, 1993, p. 5.

27 Jörg Magenau, "'Literatur ist etwas Triebhaftes': Gespräch mit dem Schriftsteller Wolfgang Hilbig," *Die Tageszeitung*, 5246, June 7–8, 1997.

28 Magenau, "Literatur ist etwas Triebhaftes."

29 Dunja Welke, "'Wenn ich gelitten habe, dann ebenso wie die anderen': Gespräch mit dem Schriftsteller Wolfgang Hilbig," *Freitag*, 21, May 17, 1991.

30 Karim Saab, "'Die DDR-Literatur hatte völlig resigniert': ein Gespräch mit Wolfgang Hilbig," in Uwe Wittstock (ed.), *Wolfgang Hilbig: Materialien zu Leben und Werk* (Frankfurt: S. Fischer, 1994), pp. 222–228; p. 228.

31 Wolfgang Hilbig, "Wie wir zu DDR-Bürgern wurden: kritische Anmerkungen zur deutschen Vereinigung," *Freitag*, 6, January 31, 1997, p. 9.

Bibliography

Adorno, Theodor W., *Ästhetische Theorie*. Gesammelte Schriften, Vol. VII, Frankfurt: Suhrkamp, 1997.
——*Negative Dialektik*, Gesammelte Schriften, Vol. VI, Frankfurt: Suhrkamp, 1997.
——*Musikalische Schriften I–III*, Gesammelte Schriften, Vol. XVI, Frankfurt: Suhrkamp, 1997.
Adorno, Theodor W. and Max Horkheimer, *Dialektik der Aufklärung*, Gesammelte Schriften, Vol. III, Frankfurt: Suhrkamp, 1997.
Bohrer, Karl-Heinz, *Plötzlichkeit: zum Augenblick des ästhetischen Scheins*, Frankfurt: Suhrkamp, 1981.
Böttiger, Helmut, "Dichtung als Geheimdienst," *Frankfurter Rundschau*, February 5, 1994, pp. ZB 2.
——"Der Schatten der Existenz, der Genitiv des Menschen," *Frankfurter Rundschau*, August 14, 1993, pp. ZB 4.
——"Ein großer Naiver," *Frankfurter Rundschau*, April 18, 1997, p. 9.
Corino, Karl, "Hölderlin aus Sachsen," *Stuttgarter Zeitung*, December 19, 1983, p. 11.
Dewey, John, *Art as Experience*, New York: Capricorn, 1958.
Geißler, Cornelia, "Cambert, der Spitzel stinkt," *Berliner Zeitung*, October 6, 1993, p. 5.
Gohlis, Tobias, "Das Leben–ein Traum der Staatssicherheit," *Stuttgarter Zeitung*, October 5, 1993, p. 1.
Habermas, Jürgen, *Strukturwandel der Öffentlichkeit: Untersuchungen zu einer Kategorie der bürgerlichen Gesellschaft*, 5th edn, with a new foreword, Frankfurt: Suhrkamp, 1990.
——*Kultur und Kritk*, Frankfurt: Suhrkamp, 1973.
——*Zur Rekonstruktion des historischen Materialismus*, Frankfurt: Suhrkamp, 1976.
——*The Theory of Communicative Action, Volume I: Reason and the Rationalization of Society*, introduction and translation by Thomas McCarthy. Originally published as *Theorie des kommunikativen Handelns: Handlungsrationalität und gesellschaftliche Rationalisierung*, in 1981 by Suhrkamp Verlag, Frankfurt.
——*The Theory of Communicative Action, Volume II: Lifeworld and System: A Critique of Functionalist Reason*, translated by Thomas McCarthy. Originally published as *Theorie des kommunikativen Handelns: Zur Kritik der funktionalistischen Vernunft*, in 1981 by Suhrkamp Verlag, Frankfurt.
——*Moralbewußtsein und kommunikatives Handeln*, Frankfurt: Suhrkamp, 1983.
——*Der philosophische Diskurs der Moderne*, Frankfurt: Suhrkamp, 1985.

——*Nachmetaphysisches Denken,* Frankfurt: Suhrkamp, 1988.

——*Die nachholende Revolution: politische Schriften VII,* Frankfurt: Suhrkamp, 1990.

——*Die Vergangenheit als Zukunft,* Munich: Piper, 1993.

——*Die Normalität einer Berliner Republik: politische Schriften VIII,* Frankfurt: Suhrkamp, 1995.

——*Die postnationale Konstellation: politische Essays,* Frankfurt: Suhrkamp, 1998.

Hilbig, Wolfgang, *Ich,* Frankfurt: S. Fischer, 1993.

——*Abwesenheit,* Frankfurt: S. Fischer, 1983.

——*Alte Abdeckerei,* Frankfurt: S. Fischer, 1991.

——"Wie wir zu DDR-Bürgern wurden: kritische Anmerkungen zur deutschen Vereinigung," *Freitag,* January 31, 1997, p. 9.

Hohendahl, Peter Uwe, *Literarische Kultur im Zeitalter des Liberalismus 1830–1870,* Munich: C.H. Beck, 1985.

Honneth, Axel, "Martin Seels *Kunst der Entzweiung,*" *Merkur,* 40 (3) (1986): 240–45.

Jauß, Hans Robert, *Ästhetische Erfahrung und literarische Hermeneutik,* Frankfurt: Suhrkamp, 1982.

Koppe, Franz, *Grundbegriffe der Ästhetik,* Frankfurt: Suhrkamp, 1983.

Kunisch, Hans Peter, "Lust an der Freiheit, die ich meine," *Süddeutsche Zeitung,* March 18, 1998, p. 20.

Löwenthal, Leo, *Das bürgerliche Bewußtsein in der Literatur,* Gesammelte Schriften, Vol. II, Frankfurt: Suhrkamp, 1981.

Magenau, Jörg, "'Literatur ist etwas Triebhaftes': Gespräch mit dem Schriftsteller Wolfgang Hilbig," *die tageszeitung,* June 7–8, 1997, n.p.

Marcuse, Herbert, *Kultur und Gesellschaft I,* Frankfurt: Suhrkamp, 1965.

Ohmann, Richard, "Speech Acts and the Definition of Literature," *Philosophy and Rhetoric,* 4 (1971): 1–19.

Rathenow, Lutz, "In den Kellern," *Die Welt,* October 5, 1993, p. 4.

Saab, Karim, "'Die DDR-Literatur hatte völlig resigniert': ein Gespräch mit Wolfgang Hilbig," in Uwe Wittstock (ed.), *Wolfgang Hilbig: Materialien zu Leben und Werk,* Frankfurt: S. Fischer, 1994, pp. 222–228.

Schirrmacher, Frank, "Wir waren der Schatten des Lebens, wir waren der Tod," *Frankfurter Allgemeine Zeitung,* October 5, 1993, p. L1.

Seel, Martin, *Die Kunst der Entzweiung: zum Begriff der ästhetischen Rationalität,* Frankfurt: Suhrkamp, 1985.

——"Kunst, Wahrheit und Welterschließung," *Perspektiven der Kunstphilosophie: Texte und Diskussionen,* ed. Franz Koppe, Frankfurt: Suhrkamp, 1991, pp. 36–80.

Taylor, Charles, "Sprache und Gesellschaft," in Axel Honneth and Hans Joas (eds), *Kommunikatives Handeln: Beiträge zu Jürgen Habermas' Theorie des kommunikativen Handelns,* Frankfurt: Suhrkamp, 1986, pp. 35–52.

Törne, Dorothea von, "Wie eine Ratte im Labyrinth," *Neue Zeit,* September 4, 1993, p. 14.

Welke, Dunje, "'Wenn ich gelitten habe, dann ebenso wie die anderen': Gespräch mit dem Schriftsteller Wolfgang Hilbig," *Freitag,* May 17, 1991.

Wellmer, Albrecht, *Zur Dialektik von Moderne und Postmoderne: Vernunftkritik nach Adorno,* Frankfurt: Suhrkamp, 1985.

Wittstock, Uwe (ed.) *Wolfgang Hilbig: Materialien zu Leben und Werk,* Frankfurt: S. Fischer, 1994.

Wolf, Christa, *Auf dem Weg nach Tabou: Texte 1990–1994,* Munich: Luchterhand, 1995.

Index

Lightning Source UK Ltd.
Milton Keynes UK
UKHW020719191122
412464UK00026B/363